10-Minute Housekeeping

10-Minute Housekeeping

Hundreds of Easy Tips to
Clean and Straighten Every Room
of Your House—Even When
You Don't Have Time

ROSE R. KENNEDY

FAIR WINDS
PRESS
GLOUCESTER, MASSACHUSETTS

Text © 2006 by Fair Winds Press

First published in the USA in 2006 by
Fair Winds Press, a member of
Quayside Publishing Group
33 Commercial Street
Gloucester, MA 01930

10 09 08 07 06   1 2 3 4 5

ISBN 1-59233-177-7

Library of Congress Cataloging-in-Publication Data
Kennedy, Rose R., 1961-
  10-minute housekeeping : hundreds of easy tips to clean and straighten every room of your house-even when you don't have time / Rose R. Kennedy.
     p. cm.
 ISBN 1-59233-177-7 (pbk.)
 1. House cleaning. 2. Housekeeping. I. Title: Ten-minute housekeeping. II. Title.
 TX324.K45 2006
  648--dc22

                                                                2005028616

Book design by Anne Gram
Cover illustration by Liz Cornaro

Printed and bound in USA

To my mother, Joanne Scott Kennedy, who along with her
many writing accomplishments and spiritual quests has
always made her home a pleasant and reflective place to be,
from the admiring apple that fell far from that tree.

How to Use This Book

The chapters in this book are arranged in three parts. Part One, "Getting Ready," tells you how to get into the mind-set for 10-minute cleaning and gives you down-and-dirty tips for dealing with the occasion those of us with less-than-spotless houses fear most: guests on the way. In Part Two, "Clean All Over," you'll find hundreds of tips on how to clean everything, from the best techniques for floors and windows to dealing with dust, mildew, and other allergens. Turn to Part Three, "Inside and Out," and you'll find tips and techniques that are especially useful for certain rooms, from the kitchen and bathroom to the porch and hallway.

I share a lot of my own hard-won tips here, but I'm not an expert on everything! So I've turned to people who are—the sort of "everyday experts" who deal with certain types of cleaning challenges over and over, whether it's the owner of a Merry Maids franchise talking about the best cleaning products or a nurse talking about how to sanitize a bathroom. Like me, you'll benefit from their expert advice—and learn quite a few insider secrets along the way!

Within each chapter, look for the boxed tips. They give you special advice that's super helpful and often the opposite of what you'd expect. Here's an overview of what you'll find:

*

10 Minutes of Prevention. Anytime 10 minutes now will keep you from hours of work later, look for the "10 Minutes of Prevention" heading. Pay attention, and you can cut cleaning time on everything from toilets and tubs to outdoor-furniture cushions and slow cookers.

*

Clean and Green. Frugal folks and those who are environmentally conscious will particularly appreciate these tips, which include anything from using vinegar in place of a chemical rinse agent in the dishwasher to cleaning the sink with baking soda. But even if you're not the type who usually heads for the environmentally friendly labels, check out these tips—lots of times, the green way is also the most effective, the cheapest, and the fastest.

＊

Once-a-Year Wonders. Even the larger-scale housekeeping chores in your home, like the ones you'll find detailed in the "Once-a-Year Wonders" boxes, can be broken down into much more manageable 10-minute projects. These tips will help you divide and conquer your most intimidating tasks.

＊

Proceed with Caution. "Safety first" is a motto for this book, and everyone should read and heed tips labeled "Proceed with Caution." They'll let you know if a product is potentially harmful to you or the thing you're cleaning, what the best (or worst) cleaner is for a specific appliance, and even if you're just going to wear out your vacuum a few months earlier if you don't heed the tip's advice.

＊

Shift Gears. These tips turn accepted cleaning wisdom on its head—and the result is quicker cleaning for you. Our everyday experts will tell you things like it's okay to hide things to keep tidy, that you shouldn't have a recycling bin for paper in your home office, and that you should run a half load of dishes.

*

Time-Saving Supplies. From a multipurpose scuff remover from the hardware store to window-cleaning fluid from the automotive department, you can pick up lots of supplies and tools on your daily errand rounds. Save time and get great results!

It Only Takes 10 Minutes

In a "how-to" writing career that spans some twenty years, I have written firsthand articles on topics from "How to Raise a Polite Child" to "How to Cook a Coca-Cola Pot Roast in the Slow Cooker." But never before now have I been able to tell readers with such complete confidence, "If this worked for me, it will work for you."

That's because while I may have a slight advantage with docile kids or cheap cuts of meat, where cleaning is concerned, my household is one of those worst-case scenarios.

There are five of us in this standard two-story 1940s-issue suburban dwelling—three teenage girls, me, and Wade, the man of the house, who makes his living in grassy, dirty lawn care. Previous inhabitants have included a St. Bernard, an archeology assistant, and a wood-burning stove, along with a succession of soccer players, horse aficionados, boisterous stray dogs, and collectors of musty books, and all have left their grubby mark. We've got lots of dust and grime—the kind with staying power. What we don't have is time: Both adults have full-time jobs, and the girls are on the extracurricular go-round. And sad to say, even though I was raised in the proverbial house so clean you could eat off the floor (with *eight* children, I might add), I've just never had the desire to spend a lot of time cleaning. Like the comedienne Roseanne, I'm waiting for them to develop a riding vacuum before I really get into it. I'm more the type who's hoping to win the lottery, so I can afford to have someone else clean the cat boxes, mop the floors, and clean those little dead moths out of the porch light.

So far, that hasn't happened. Instead, I've learned to develop 10-minute housecleaning techniques, drawing from decades of life experience. If an idea doesn't work at my house, where the contents of the bottom shelf of the refrigerator door are held in with a bungee cord and the newspaper is spread over six rooms at the end of the day, I didn't include it here. Nor will you find deep-cleaning methods between these covers—if it takes more than 10 minutes, it's been banished.

Trust me, you *can* make your home cleaner and nicer, working just 10 minutes at a time. Let me repeat, "If it worked for me, it will work for you." These tips will help you stay on top of the little jobs so they don't turn into those tough ones that make you want to hop the next train and file for divorce on the way out of town. And if you ever do muster up the budget for some cleaning help, you'll be able to extend the clean feel much longer. Every tool or technique in this book is the stuff of real life, tested in a home where people raise their voices when they're arguing about who will unload the dishwasher, and most everybody has to beg, borrow, and steal to find matching clean socks on a school morning. I'm right here with you, so if I say 10 minutes will take care of some scratches on wood furniture, or not to ever buy seat cushions that can't come off and go in the wash, you can take me at my word. If you can't trust a woman in her forties who still uses Mr. Bubble instead of aromatherapy bath oil beads in the tub because Mr. B won't leave a ring, who can you trust?

Most of the advice in the first two chapters, "Changing Your Mind-Set" and "Guests on the Way," comes straight from my personal experience. In later chapters, you'll also get the benefit of advice from dozens of "everyday experts" I've been privileged to get to know, from a hardware superstore's lighting department manager who gives the lowdown on cleaning chandeliers to a longtime soccer coach who told me how to get scuff marks off of linoleum.

With our combined efforts, you'll come to understand what makes a 10-minute job a 10-minute job, which dependable products you can pick up at your favorite discount department store or along with the groceries, which fad cleaning supplies live up to the hype, and which long-held cleaning laws are actually urban myths. Who knew, for example, that a wall is the one thing you don't want to wash from top to bottom, or that you shouldn't keep a handy trash can next to the computer for recyclable paper?

There are a few tips I've gleaned from living at this house that didn't make the grade for the book. I figured, for example, that few people would need to share my serendipitous revelation that green Fruitopia poured into a burnt Farberware saucepan that has been hanging around in the garden for a month would clear the crud off so completely that it would be fit to heat SpaghettiOs in once again, even if it has lost its handle. Everyone should be aware that mixing chlorine and ammonia produces dangerous fumes, but I don't guess anyone has to know that Wade, after a failure to communicate with the resident cleaning-book author, mopped the floor with ammonia just days after I'd wiped off a few spots with a Clorox wipe, and this just hours before a handful of family members were stopping by to carpool to my nephew's graduation. Were we ever glad to have fans, windows, air conditioners, and people so polite they pretended they preferred to chat in the driveway until we all left.

There are lots of cleaning lessons learned in every household, and I feel like hundreds of the best ones have made their way from my house and the homes of these everyday experts onto these pages.

Sometimes we all need a little push to start the cleaning process. Chapter 2, "Guests on the Way," is inspired by the panic we all feel when people are coming over to visit and, we suspect, judge our households. We're particularly guilty at our house of doing most of our "making nice" because other people are coming over, and we blamed Wade's dad for our disarray through all of 2003 because he skipped his annual weekend visit that year.

But it's also really nice to do a little extra cleaning just for the family. Treat yourself for a change—take the hairspray off the bathroom mirror, wipe down the kitchen cabinets with a bit of water and vinegar or put a cinnamon stick in the vacuum-cleaner bag so everything smells delicious. So many little cleaning jobs make things a little neater and make life a little sweeter. I know, because I've tried them. And if it works for me, it can work for you.

Rose R. Kennedy

Table of Contents

How to Use This Book

Introduction: It Only Takes 10 Minutes

Part One: Getting Ready

Chapter 1.   Changing Your Mindset   23
Chapter 2.   Guests on the Way   45

Part Two: Clean All Over

Chapter 3.   Caring for Floors and Carpets   69
Chapter 4.   Window-Cleaning Wisdom   79
Chapter 5.   Dealing with Dust, Mildew,
              and Other Allergens   93
Chapter 6.   Let There Be (Clean) Lights   109

✳

Part Three: Inside and Out

Chapter 7.   Livable Living Rooms,
             Functional Family Rooms   119
Chapter 8.   A Cleaner Kitchen   139
Chapter 9.   The Bacteria-Free Bathroom   167
Chapter 10. The Better-Kept Bedroom   191
Chapter 11. The Clean, Organized Home Office   209
Chapter 12. A Clean Porch to Perch On   223
Chapter 13. Tidy Exits, Entries, and Hallways 239

Part One

Getting Ready

Chapter 1

Changing Your Mindset

Old habits die hard, and that's the biggest obstacle to overcome when you're cleaning 10 minutes at a time. But I don't mean quirks like throwing clothes on the bedroom floor or not really caring that there are dust bunnies under the living-room couch. While those habits won't speed you along when you attempt some 10-minute cleaning, they won't put you at a severe disadvantage, either.

Instead, becoming a successful 10-minute housecleaner requires cleaning up some *mental* habits. First, you'll have to stop trying so hard and setting such high standards. Maybe you're like me and really know how to do the deep cleaning: wiping baseboards, polishing toasters, reorganizing the attic. But when you can dedicate only a few minutes at a time to cleaning, you'll have to give up on the idea that you'll get those big (or deep) cleaning jobs done and focus on the ones you can do quickly and well.

I came across a reassuring message in another book, the *Woman's Home Companion Household*. "Wholesale spring cleaning stamps a housewife as out-of-date and inefficient, and causes undue stress on the entire household," it said. And guess what? That book was published in 1948! Of course, their ideas of "wholesale spring cleaning" would probably stagger any of us modern mortals, but the message is there: divide and conquer; think small. And most importantly, our first principle of 10-minute housecleaning: **Attempt only those jobs you can really achieve in 10 minutes.**

Set Realistic Expectations

The second new habit to form is not to feel bad that you're not accomplishing more. I can remember years ago when I had a demanding job that often required me to bring projects home on the weekend. After suffering through several Sundays, my husband made a rule: I had to finish the work on Friday. While that didn't make the work take any less time, it completely eliminated the ceaseless hours I spent worrying about doing the work before Monday rolled around again, which drained energy not just from me, but from our entire household.

That message applies here, too. Instead of investing a single second worrying about the curtains you hung up without pressing or hearing the siren song of the mildew in the basement, spend all the time you can spare working. It's easier on your psyche, and it's more productive, too. The key to this thinking? Instead of comparing your cleaning efforts to those of your friend who needs only four hours of sleep or to some remembered spotless place from your upbringing, adopt the second principle of 10-minute housecleaning: **Be happy that while your house will never be all clean, if you chip away at it, the parts of the house that matter most to you will always be clean.**

Don't Focus on Supplies

And here's another essential component of the mind-set for 10-minute housecleaning: Keep in mind that there is no such thing as one essential supply. You can always find something to clean in 10 minutes and something to clean it with, even if all you have is some warm water and a paper towel (or a coffee filter if you've run out of paper towels).

Particularly when you're a rookie 10-minute cleaner, focus on little jobs you can finish off with supplies you already have on hand. Use a piece of old flannel shirt to dust the piano, for example, instead of racing off to purchase a special product so you can clean the toilet. In some cases, you might have to dig deep. But try a wad of discarded nylon pantyhose as a sponge if all your sponges smell of mildew, or use white vinegar on a soft cloth if you've run out of glass cleaner or all-purpose spray.

Buying new cleaning supplies is, in fact, one of the top hindrances to actually getting something done—you're there at store looking for a Magic Eraser when you could be home washing the porch with the garden hose, or you're too tired to settle down to do some actual cleaning, even for 10 minutes, because you've made a special trip to the store. It's a lot like making a list, as far as I'm concerned. For people like me, the simple act of writing down what you need to do somehow makes you feel like you've already done it. If you concentrate on what you need to buy to clean, you may neglect to do the actual cleaning.

The same goes for homemade concoctions. Even the completely effective, environmentally sound ones aren't worth making if mixing up a batch is going to be the only thing you accomplish—that, or a trip to the store to buy teak oil or whatever ingredient you're missing. When you have the time and the ingredients, sure, go for the green. Otherwise, particularly when you're first trying to get into the 10-minute-cleaning mind-set, keep our third principle in mind: **Never obsess about supplies — work with what you have on hand or whatever's convenient.**

Of course, there are products that are workhorses, not gimmicks, and you should definitely seek them out. A microfiber duster, for example, is everything it claims to be: environmentally friendly, washable, and a veritable dust magnet. Lots of other trendy items are discussed later in the book under the heading "Time-Saving Supplies." But in your initial efforts at 10-minute cleaning, don't get too hung up on supplies. It might distract you from having those all-important first 10-minute successes. Later, when you've at least tried a few of the simple "soap and water" jobs, there will be plenty of time to invest in, say, a Swiffer dust mop or a big box of Arm & Hammer washing soda.

Getting to Work

There is a fourth habit you will want to develop, and it is the only one that doesn't involve reducing expectations. But first let me tell you about a message board I came across on the Internet while doing some research for one of these chapters. A few posts in, I realized that these homemakers weren't asking for tips or sharing cleaning methods, they were reeling off how many chores they'd done that day. Some of them

(I am not making this up) were things like, "washed the windows in the basement, pushed the refrigerator aside to mop underneath it, and plan to soak the stove burners before lunch."

Whew! I could hardly close the screen fast enough. Not that I don't support people's rights to be obsessed with housework if they want, or to pursue it as a hobby. It's just that 10-minute housecleaning doesn't apply to people like that. I can't imagine that you're trying to finish off some housework so you'll have time for . . . more housework.

Instead, I'm assuming that you need more tips that will work in the limited time you have for cleaning. The goal here isn't to make housecleaning a second identity or a competition, just to help you become fairly competent if you weren't born into an "eat off the floor" dynasty, or to help you make wise use of your time with some ingenious shortcuts and workhorse cleaning concoctions if you already know your way around the mop and pail but could use some new ideas—or some new motivation. It's kind of like the "one day at a time" slogan of AA: just pledge to do the 10 minutes, then move on to another 10-minute chore if you feel like it. And here's where you need to escalate your expectations to adopt the fourth principle of 10-minute housecleaning:

Realize how much you can do in 10 minutes. There are so many ways to make use of 10-minute increments, from reorganizing that annoying medicine cabinet with the contents that topple out every time you open the door to flipping the mattress, getting crayon marks off the wall, or cleaning the chandelier. This book is full of hundreds of ideas, and the beauty of it all is that you are entirely free to choose which jobs you want to do when you have 10 minutes available. Of course, there are ways to make even better use of your time than simply following the tips in the book. Consider these ideas:

✳

Pick what you can do easily. A few years back, a company paid a lot of money to send me to a seminar where we took some quizzes to pinpoint our work styles. I was shocked to hear that my response, "I do the easiest task first," did not make me an efficient worker. Seems that other criteria, such as which job is the most urgent, should hold sway in the executive world. That's not the case here, though. If it makes you feel good to get something done and out of the way, do that first, even if it's not the most critical task at hand.

✳

Set yourself up. You can also choose to spend your 10 minutes preparing materials for another job. But as a rule, do this only if the prep yields a tool you can use at least three other times. A good example is making homemade wipes. Sure, you can buy them, but that trip to the store will probably take more than 10 minutes, or you might have the furniture-polish kind when you want to clean tile, and so forth. In place of a purchased product, fold half a roll's worth of heavy-duty paper towels such as Brawny into fourths, layering them into a square or rectangular plastic container (such as Gladware), and then pour 1/2 cup (120 ml) of pine cleaner mixed with 2 cups (475 ml) of water over the top. Voila! You have wipes you can use in the bathroom or on kitchen counters and cabinets, or keep handy for telephone receivers and door knobs. Particularly under the heading "Clean and Green," there are dozens of ideas throughout the book for easy-to-make cleaning solutions and tools.

Consider sweating the small stuff. Another possibility is starting with the little jobs that might turn into big jobs if you wait to do them later. This is a really good strategy for the type A's among us (and yes, I'm one of those, too) who simply can't bear to waste time or money. For example, merely running a little cold water in bowls or glasses that have held milk keeps you from scrubbing and soaking them later—or constantly reaching into the cabinet for a glass, only to grab one with that telltale milk ring on it. Switching to natural soaps helps keep the bathtub from getting intolerable rings—or necessitating strong bleach or hours of scrubbing. In fact, if you strive for efficiency, make sure to check out the "10 Minutes of Prevention" tips throughout this book: They make such good use of your time that you may be able to work in a few more jobs!

Work where you can do the most good. Another possibility for those of us who strive for efficiency is to choose 10-minute tasks that will have the highest impact. A good example is changing the furnace filter or cleaning the filter on the air conditioner or dehumidifier. That will prevent a lot of dust and dirt from accumulating in the house, so it cuts down on several different dusting and cleaning tasks.

A lot of this "most good" aspect depends on you and your house. In my abode, for example, any time or money spent on keeping the cats from spraying has the greatest payoff, since it cuts back on pushed-over plants, carpet cleaning, and endless rounds of laundry, and it makes the animals happier, too. That means I buy a $38 product called Feliway, which looks and works like a Plug-In air freshener, and successfully uses chemicals to fool my kitties into thinking they've already sprayed! Pricey, yes, but it takes only a minute to install and prevents at least a couple of hours of work when the cats are stressed, so to me it's worth every penny. I'm sure there are similar situations in your own house, whether they have to do with keeping the dishes and fridge clean so you don't have to eat out as often, the kids' rooms picked up so they can have visitors, or the home office in acceptable shape so you don't have to pay someone else to find the records and do the taxes. In general, if you're indecisive about where to start with a 10-minute cleaning task, try to take on whatever will have the greatest impact.

✳

Neaten strategically. If you have the type of clutter personality where you prefer for things to look tidy but can overlook dirt, you might want to clean the item that will instantly make things look neater first. In the living room, a person like you should start with the sofa, picking up crumbs with a hand-held vacuum and then plumping the pillows and folding the throws. In the bedroom, spend your 10 minutes making the bed. In an eating area, you'll probably want to clear off the eating surface and maybe toss a nice tablecloth on top.

Figure out what you'd like to hire out. There, I said it. It's a perfectly reasonable goal to want to hire someone else to clean your house. But you know what? You'll still have to do some stuff yourself. And there are bound to be a few tasks that you're too embarrassed to expect hired help to take on. (I envision my sister Cathy, back when she was an engineer in Salt Lake City, Utah, blithely telling me she needed to get off the phone so she could "clean for the cleaning lady.") And a few you wouldn't entrust to anyone else, like dusting your priceless collection of prehistoric Chinese jade figurines. So, if hiring help is a possibility, choose your 10-minute tasks with an eye toward figuring out what you don't like that someone else might be willing to do for pay, and getting the house in decent enough shape that a cleaning service would be willing to come in to do the deep cleaning. And if you find a few jobs you don't mind doing yourself, that will give you more options when you hire someone—tell them you're happy to vacuum and dust, for example, if they'll pay extra attention to cleaning the shower or the counters.

Choose what's important to you. Another friend got criticized by her mother for taking the time to neatly braid the spent leaves on her daffodils (a trick I think she picked up from Martha Stewart) when her three kids' playroom was piled high with junk and she hadn't folded the laundry yet. But you know what? There's always going to be a backlog of chores, so you can't let that stop you from getting something done. And if it's something you can really appreciate and take satisfaction from, it shouldn't matter that it's not what someone else in your position might choose to do. If you prefer to spend your time, for example, giving your lamps a nice dusting while ignoring the dishes in the sink, that's up to you.

Work with the fates. This is probably the only time in choosing a task that you shouldn't exercise complete freedom of choice. Don't, I repeat, *do not*, bother to do a job right now if it would be so much simpler to do it another time. One chore that springs to mind is washing screens. Simply put it off if you can't comfortably do it outside—rinsing screens in the tub doesn't really get the job done, and it creates loads more work in the form of wet floors, dirty towels, and grimy hands on indoor walls. You get the picture. A few other don'ts include cleaning the oven during the day if people are home, washing windows on a sunny day, and defrosting the refrigerator when it's hot out.

✳

Tune out distractions. When you're cleaning, the impulse, of course, is to pick up as you go along, rearrange, and toss unneeded stuff. Resist the temptation. You can't complete a 10-minute task when you're trying to simultaneously declutter and deep clean. Instead, follow these rules:

✔ If an area's cluttered, pick up first, then clean if there's time. Otherwise, it takes forever to dust or vacuum, because you're constantly moving stuff from side to side or trying to figure out where it belongs.

✔ Place all displaced items in one box or bag and then return them to their homes another time—or at the end of the task if you have time. Commuting back and forth with found objects eats up all your time.

✔ If you're just quick cleaning, don't pull out furniture in order to vacuum behind it or pull up cushions to vacuum beneath them.

✔ Split decluttering and cleaning into two distinct chores—never pause to toss out unwanted magazines when your objective is to tidy the coffee table, for example.

✔ Don't stop to pay bills when you're cleaning the office.

✔ Don't water the plants when you're in the middle of cleaning a room.

✔ If you can get away with it, don't answer the phone while you're cleaning-especially if you really are limiting your tasks to just 10 minutes apiece.

✔ Never start a new chore in the middle of another one. You'd be amazed at how quickly you can finish a job once you begin—and how long it takes to gear back up again if you pause.

Making Time to Clean

Sometimes it seems impossible to find even 10 minutes for cleaning. But it's not—even in today's superbusy, superstressed world. Here are some ways to make the most of your cleaning time by getting creative. You can do it!

✳

Browse this book instead of mail-order catalogs. If you're fond of perusing glossies with stuff you can't afford that would probably just clutter up your house anyway, get in the habit of flipping through *10-Minute Housekeeping* while you relax instead. Haul out the Post-its and tag things that you might try the next time you have 10 minutes.

✳

Set it to music. If you like to listen to music while you work, burn a CD that groups songs into 10-minute "sets." When the 10-minute set ends, you can turn to another task or stop.

*

Try 10-minute phone calls. Do two good things at once by calling friends you're out of touch with for a conversation that will last, you got it, 10 minutes. Of course, you can clean at the same time because you've invested in a hands-free phone. If you're smart, you'll set a kitchen timer for the call, or get your friend to do 10-minute jobs on her end, too.

*

Photocopy chores for the family. If other members of the family can read, they can be in on this. I'm not suggesting that your eleven-year-old son read this book, but you can photocopy ten or twenty of the tips that you know will work at your house. Cut them into strips and keep them in a job jar that anyone can access, or make each person their own age- and interest-specific jar.

Aim for 10 minutes of work, 10 minutes of reward. Whether you're trying to motivate yourself or some reluctant family members, come up with some rewards that are fitting for 10 minutes of labor. At my house, the first 10 minutes a day is its own reward. After that, a motivator for kids could be an exchange of 10 minutes of cleaning for 10 minutes of video games, or getting to stay up 10 minutes later per job from the book. Consider offering double rewards for jobs done when guests are on the way, or done before 9 a.m. if you have difficulty getting the family up and working on the weekend. For guys, the video games might work, too, or 10 minutes' extra sleep in the morning. If you're the mom and have to make the rewards come true, make sure that your own motivator is something someone else can provide: a 10-minute pedicure every 10 chores, for example, or 10 minutes with a book and a latte come next Saturday morning.

Drop everything and clean. I was so impressed with the public middle school my daughter and stepdaughter attended this past year. It insisted that every student in the school of more than a thousand always have some recreational reading at the ready. Then, randomly, but at least once a week, the whole school would "drop everything and read" for 15 or 20 minutes. This same approach is perfect for the hectic household. Every now and again when most everyone's home, insist on "dropping everything to clean," but only for 10 minutes! Don't try this during the final episode of your favorite TV drama, naturally, but do insist that everyone participate, even the folks with a term paper due the next day or that husband of yours who's trying to skulk out to the den with his crossword puzzle.

Occasionally, wrap up the session with, say, frozen yogurt or a great video, but just as often, make the cleaning just part of everyday responsibilities. Not only will you multiply your effectiveness by the number of family members in your household, but you can show everyone (including yourself) just how much you can accomplish in 10 minutes!

Ready to get started? Turn the page to start finding out how to get your house clean—10 minutes at a time!

Chapter 2

Guests on the Way

Don't panic! Guests can mean stress, especially if they're last-minute or you just haven't had a minute to get the house ready. To make sure you get to enjoy your guests' visits, make the most of the prep time you have. When the whole house is dirty, prioritize what you can get done to make it better—or, at least, make it *seem* better—before guests arrive. Read on for ways to get your home guest-ready, 10 minutes at a time.

*

Adopt a Scottish philosophy regarding unannounced visits. Susan Crawford, a very dear friend of mine here in Knoxville, Tennessee, recently made an extended trip to her husband's home country of Scotland. There, friends and relatives had a motto about visiting that really appealed to her: "If you're coming to see me, drop by anytime. If you're coming to see the house, make an appointment." If you like, cross-stitch this onto a pillow, but at the very least, adopt the idea and spread the word to close family and friends so they know what to expect at your house. That takes a lot of the tension out of responding to unexpected guests, and even when you know someone's stopping by and the house is nowhere near clean and inviting, you can comfort yourself with the idea that you're focusing on what's really important: time with friends.

*

Visit your own home first. Susan Castle, my brother-in-law's wife and an inspiringly organized woman who lives in Chattanooga, Tennessee, has lots of experience with drop-in guests, namely the potential clients who come by one of the three BodyLite (LA Weight Loss) franchises she and husband Rich Castle own and manage. "Every once in a while I sit in the reception area at the store and pretend I'm a guest and ask myself, 'What do I see?'" she says. "I do that at home, too, and it's a good way to see how ugly that stack of papers in the corner is, or notice that the cushions have dog hair that might make someone with allergies uncomfortable."

*

Skip guest hand towels and soap. Don't spend any of your precious time coming up with neat little embossed guest hand towels or those festive soaps—no one will use them, and your time is better spent making sure the family towels and soap are in good shape, because people will inevitably use them to wash and dry their hands.

Beware of weary travelers. A lot of Susan Castle's relatives live within a few hours' drive, and she's frequently the hostess when they get together. There's a dual trap to avoid when guests have been driving, she says. "Don't hide extra junk in the guest room, or someone's bound to arrive and say, 'I'm not feeling well from the drive, can I lie down?'" Just as important, make sure you have a bed with a clean pillow available for weary travelers, particularly if there are kids in the party.

Shift Gears

✔ **Have people over as often as you can.** While it seems like that would involve oodles more cleaning, it will actually save you time because you'll be more likely to do the little chores—like wiping down the toilet rim or getting all the drinking glasses really clean—often, and that's always easier than waiting until they're big jobs and trying to tackle, say, a crusty microwave or grimy tub with an hour to go before your boss and his wife pull in the driveway. Plus you'll know who's perfectly comfortable being entertained family-style at your slightly messy house, instead of building up great expectations (and huge cleaning jobs) for a once-a-year soiree.

Stop half an hour before. Even if you're not through, stop cleaning a half hour before you expect guests to arrive. That way, you'll have time for a shower—and for the telltale smell of Pine-Sol to dissipate a little! More important, you won't get caught with the dust mop in hand when Aunt Edna arrives 10 minutes early, and guests won't be roaming the house unattended (and heading straight for the place where you stashed all those muddy boots) while you're trying to transition to the "host" role.

Don't worry about the "first impression" porch or foyer. This is good advice anytime, but particularly when guests will be arriving after dark. Since you're on a tight schedule, don't spend a lot of time on the areas where you and your guests will just be breezing through for a moment or two. Instead, focus your efforts on the room where they'll spend the majority of the visit.

Don't kid yourself about the kitchen. You can dust and polish the dining room table and set it with lavish china, or vacuum the rec room floor, curtains, and couch cushions, but don't delude yourself that your guests will obediently stay in those areas while you cook and serve from the incredibly untidy kitchen. Most guests worthy of entertaining will want to be in the kitchen with you, offering to help or chatting with you while you work, so don't make that the place you hide great bundles of kids' toys or neglect to mop, figuring no one will notice. And make sure you've got an extra chair or two in the kitchen, and an extra chore for anyone who wants to tarry there with you—they'll be too busy chopping the parsley or washing the stemware to worry about that grease on the cabinet doors!

*

Keep people in the clean spaces. Along the same lines, don't just assume the guests will hang out in the areas of the house that look best and are most sanitary because that's what you're expecting. They invariably gravitate to the messy spots, and I know at my house, the lure of the cat's bathroom is almost palpable. Even if I've spent 30 minutes getting the convenient downstairs bathroom sweet smelling and sparkly, someone will invariably settle on the bathroom with the litter box, which my cat has certainly used in the four or five minutes since I set out a fresh one. If you're comfortable with yourself and your house, you can, of course, ask people to stay in designated areas because the rest of the house is a wreck.

*

Lure people to the clean rooms. To bolster that request or in place of it, there are other measures you can take. In weather extremes, adjust it so the room where you want people is the warmest or the coolest. Build a nice fire or burn several fat pine-scented candles in the fireplace and watch people get drawn like moths. Put the drinks or snacks in the room where you want everybody, even if you have to bring in a cooler or walk three rooms from the kitchen to do it. And, keep in mind, even if you've gotten only one room clean, you may need two-for arguing couples who need to take a break, for nursing mothers, or for guys who want to catch the game on television while everyone else plays charades. Just do your best and make sure to designate which room will take those who need a break. It should be the less appealing room. (If anyone absolutely has to watch the game, there's a television in Wade's freezing workshop outside.)

Step inside and inhale. If you're at home a lot, you might get so used to pet, mildew, or even cooking smells that you don't notice them anymore. Before guests arrive, take a walk for a few minutes and then come back in and breathe deeply (or have an objective party do it for you). Then tackle the smells as needed—opening windows, turning on fans, taking out the garbage, cleaning the debris trap in the sink, setting out small bowls of vinegar to absorb musty air, spraying a very lightly scented (linen, fresh laundry) antibacterial spray in the bathroom. Finally, if you know none of your guests has a perfume allergy, light a few lightly scented candles such as vanilla or cinnamon in the rooms where you'll be spending a lot of time.

*

Bake bread or cookies. If you have a seldom-used bread machine, a couple of hours before guests arrive is a great time to dust it off and rev it up. The smell of baking bread is tantalizing and homey and will distract guests from other smells or messes in the house. If you don't have a bread machine, try to keep a few bags of frozen bread dough on hand. If you can remember, defrost one in the morning so you can have it baking when evening guests arrive. Another great alternative (if it doesn't present too much of a temptation!): Keep a package of break-and-bake chocolate chip cookie dough on hand. You can slide a batch into the oven with just a few minutes' notice, and most guests would much rather smell baking chocolate and then nosh on warm cookies than worry about whether you have a ring in the tub or a half inch of dust on the television.

Put a cinnamon stick in the vacuum bag before that quick run-through. That way, your guests will breathe in cookie scents, not the musty air the vacuum can put out.

10 Minutes of Prevention

Try dim lighting. Entryways often have harsh, unflattering lighting that shows every cobweb and crayon mark on the wall. And strong light in the living room or dining room is great to read by, but also great to see dust by. Before guests arrive, consider switching out a few white bulbs in these areas for softer colors—pink or peach, for example, or the warm (and kind) light of an amber bulb. A dimmer's a great idea, too, or candlelight for the dinner table, but this can backfire. Ask yourself ahead of time if someone (not realizing your ploy to obscure mess and dust) might request stronger light to read or eat by. My father definitely comes to mind, and vegetarians and picky eaters might demand to be able to clearly see what they're eating.

Time-Saving Supplies

I know, I know, if you had time to keep all this stuff in stock, you'd probably have plenty of time to have the house perfectly clean when guests arrive. But if you can keep even a few of these items around, you'll be ahead of the game when people come by:

- ✓ **A disposable litter box:** This is handy only if you have cats, of course, but they do sell one-use litter boxes at most pet or discount department stores, which are helpful if you never know what smells might greet you when you get home from work—and you'll be followed by dinner guests in half an hour. Instead of toiling to change and clean the permanent litter box, whisk it out to the backyard and set out the inviting one-time-use box. If you can't find a place to buy them, consider spending 10 minutes making your own with aluminum broiler pans and some litter, and then covering them up with plastic wrap to set aside for that rainy day.

- ✓ **Extra vacuum bags or filters.** You can always fudge if you don't have quite the right cleaning or dusting spray and are expecting people over in an hour or so, but it's difficult to get by without vacuuming. If at all possible, keep a clean extra bag in a special place for just such emergencies. For the bagless models, make sure you purchase an extra filter to have on hand. When the filter gets dirty, you're basically throwing dust into the air, not getting things a bit cleaner.

✓ **Clean cloth tablecloths.** Scour linen sales and eBay for a collection of cloth tablecloths that match your decor or are superplain, and keep a stack of them freshly laundered. That way, you can toss one over a sticky table or dog-hair-covered couch at a moment's notice, for example, or use it to disguise a big pile of junk that you simply don't have time to get rid of before people arrive.

✓ **Basket o' towels for overnight guests.** This is more about money than time, but it's worth every penny if you have family members or wayfaring friends who are prone to drop by for a few nights with little or no notice. Buy and wash a couple of extra bath towels, hand towels, and washcloths; roll them up; and hide them away in a basket (even a laundry basket), along with a roll of toilet paper, a pair of clean pillowcases, and a nice new bar of soap. Next time someone shows up, you'll be ready!

Make food or games the priority. My ex-husband used to always shake his head when I went into cleaning overdrive hours before party guests arrived. "If the food is good, no one will care what the house looks like," he would tell me, and I'm surprised at how often this advice has proved true. Since you don't have much time to prepare, concentrate on providing snacks or treats that people will really like, and a really good glass of wine or special soda, and downplay the idea that your house should be perfect or even above average. Or, if you're not much into serving food, make sure you have an activity planned—several photo albums ready to leaf through, for example, or a Scrabble game set out on a lazy Susan. Or do both. Guests will look forward to having something fun to do and respond to the nurturing of their senses, and all but the most ardent neatniks will have a good time despite the dust or scuff marks on the floor. (And make a mental note not to keep inviting people who care more about how neat the house is than the company, entertainment, or snacks.)

✳

Countdown to clean. When you're having guests, it may seem like there's never enough time to prepare, but there are varying degrees of "tight on time." Depending on how long you've waited to start, or how much notice you've had before the guests are due, pick one of these "hurry up and clean" strategies:

✔ **The weekend before a visit,** you still have time to clean the toilet, sink, and floor in the bathroom, which may be the only place your guests will ever be on their own and have the time or inclination to reflect on the cleanliness of your house. If the guests will be staying overnight, also clean the shower, and wash and change the linens and towels. You should also have a chance to vacuum or sweep in whatever room(s) you plan to be spending most of your time; to get that pile of dirty dishes in the sink washed; and to make sure you've got enough really clean glasses, eating utensils, and dishes to go around. Nothing turns people off quite as much as helping themselves to glasses from the cabinet only to pull down one with baked-on dirt, dust, or a milk ring, or grabbing a fork with congealed egg yolk from the utensil drawer.

✔ **The night before,** you should still have time for the bathroom stuff. If you don't have any clean linen in the house, consider heading to a nearby Laundromat so you can wash your sheets (for overnight guests) and towels all at once, which costs about $10 but saves a couple of hours of monitoring the washer and dryer. Also set out some clean dishes if you'll be serving food, check the cat box, sweep or vacuum the primary entertainment spot, and set out some candles. Make sure you have the ingredients for whatever food you might be serving, and make it ahead if you can.

✔ **An hour before,** you still have time to do the toilet and sink. Wash any dirty dishes that smell bad and hide the rest, making sure you have a couple of clean glasses if you'll be serving drinks, and at least some decorative paper plates or substantial paper napkins if you'll be bringing out any light snacks. Go through the space where you'll be spending most of your time with an empty box or shopping bag and pick up everything that doesn't belong there. Make at least a couple of clean seats available by vacuuming them or wiping them down.

✔ **When they're coming up the walk,** wash your hands, take the litter box outside if it's not clean, and make sure you've got toilet paper and a cleanish towel in the bathroom.

✳

Resist the urge to reorganize. If you're like me, it's mighty tempting to try to clear some clutter or do a really thorough cleaning job when you start to spiff up the place for guests, if only because it's one of the few times you ever have willing helpers. Don't do it! You'll end up with a couple of neat and clean stacks of stuff and still have nowhere for the guests to sit that's not covered with magazines or dog hair.

*

Go lightly, work quickly. Try to accurately predict where you'll be spending the most time with your guests, and then vacuum and dust there, but without moving furniture or trying to remove spots in the carpet. Also, use the vacuum's upholstery attachment to run over the sofa cushions, but don't vacuum under them—that's a job for a day when no one's coming to visit at any second. Make sure to dust the coffee table, particularly if you're going to be serving from it, and arrange the magazine display neatly, but don't try to make decisions about which magazines or catalogs are staying—that takes too long.

Shift Gears

It *is* okay to hide stuff. Contrary to popular cleaning wisdom, it's okay to hide messy stuff that you don't have time to wash and/or organize if you're pressed for time. But there are ground rules. First, don't hide anything that you don't use often, or you'll never find it again and it will just add to household clutter (especially if you replace it when its time of year rolls around again). You can stash a dirty coffee maker, the dog's dish, or your monthly bills for the moment, but don't do the same with, say, strings of Christmas lights or the wok you use once a year. And make sure you hide the stuff somewhere you'll go again soon: the bathtub, coat closet, or the shower, for example, instead of the shed out back or the garage.

＊

Save nice shopping bags. One of my favorite cleaning role models, Susan Castle, also has lots of experience in retail, and she still saves those nice shopping bags with the woven or plastic handles. Then when she doesn't have time to really clean before guests arrive, she dumps unclaimed objects in the bags and sticks them in a closet until she has more leisure. "This works particularly well if you have one of those computer work centers built into the kitchen design," she says. "You just scoop all the visible stuff into one bag, and later you know you'll be able to find it because it's in there somewhere." One of these bags or a cardboard box really comes in handy for a quick cleaning of the living room or den, too. Just place any item that's out of place in the bag. Don't try to go put it back where it belongs; that will take too long or might distract you entirely from the task at hand. After the guests are gone, walk the container around and drop the items back at their rightful homes.

Part Two

Clean All Over

Chapter 3

Caring for Floors and Carpets

✳

Sweep before dusting. Brooms tend to raise dust, so wait for it to resettle before dusting the furniture.

*

Sweep or vacuum a wood floor first.

That will remove most of the surface dust and grime, and you can finish off by damp-mopping-dipping a sponge mop (or large sponge) into a bucket of plain water, squeezing it until it is almost dry, then running it over the surface of the floor. Make sure to rinse the mop well every few swipes, and squeeze it practically dry again. If you get more water on the floor than will dry itself in a couple of minutes, go back and dab it off with a clean towel or dry sponge.

Make wood floors shine with vinegar and polish. Take a second pass at damp-mopping with a mixture of 1/4 cup (60 ml) of vinegar and 1 tablespoon (15 ml) of liquid furniture polish added to 1/2 gallon (1.9 L) of water.

Proceed with Caution

Never use lemon oil on wood floors. The lemon oil attracts dust, which can make the floors slippery, says Tammy Wood of Extreme Cleaning in Arvada, Colorado.

✳

Scoot scuff marks with toothpaste. On a hardwood floor, scrub off heel or scuff marks with toothpaste and a toothbrush, then wipe the spot clean with a damp sponge and dry. On linoleum, try a little bit of baby oil or Vaseline on a clean cloth, but be sure to get up the oil afterward with a paper towel or the dry edge of the cloth.

✳

Dust-mop decisively. In spots where a broom would just move dust or animal hair around, try a dust mop. Improve its chances of success by spraying it with dusting spray (not to be confused with furniture polish). Then push it in figure eights in front of you, like a sailor swabbing the deck, making sure you never lose contact with the floor. Don't undo your hard work: When the mop has taken up all the dust it can hold, slip it into a large plastic bag to shake it off, or to carry it outside to shake into the trash can or the bushes.

Time-Saving Supplies

Lift Off scuff marks. As a longtime volunteer soccer coach and regional American Youth Soccer Organization commissioner, Shawn Simpson has plenty of experience with scuff marks from soccer cleats and other athletic shoes. "A product called Lift Off that I bought at a discount department store works great," she says. "I've also used it for crayon marks on walls, price stickers on the glass of picture frames, you name it."

Give your dust mop a haircut. If you trim about a half inch from the strands of a dust mop, it's easier to control.

Time-Saving Supplies

Swiffer lightweight mops are great. These are the ones you use to dust-mop hardwood floors, says self-proclaimed neat freak Susan Castle, who owns three dachshunds in Chattanooga, Tennessee, and spends a lot of time cleaning up dog hair. "They make it easy to get under furniture, and they pick up the dust and dog hair instead of just moving it around, like a broom would," she says. Another plus for Susan, who is stepmother to four active young adults: "Afterward, you can just throw the cloth away, instead of washing it and dealing with all that dirt a second time in the washer and dryer."

＊

Launder a dust-mop head in a mesh bag. "This keeps it from getting frizzled and hard to use," says Louise Kurzeka, who with Pam Hix co-owns Everything's Together, an organizing business in the Minneapolis area. When the mop head comes out of the washer, hang it out to air-dry. "Otherwise, it will create static electricity, and make the floors attract dust!" warns Louise.

＊

Toss throw rugs in the dryer. Instead of beating small throw rugs, toss them in the dryer on a no-heat setting for 15 minutes, and let the lint trap catch the dirt and hair.

✳

If it's been a while since you've vacuumed, get out the broom.
Sweep over your carpet first to loosen dirt and get up any big stuff. Then bring in the vacuum for the finale.

Clean and Green

Freshen carpets with baking soda. Whether you need to pick up pet odors or merely want to freshen your carpet, try ordinary baking soda before turning to the chemical or highly scented stuff. Using a baking sifter, sprinkle baking soda liberally over the carpet and let it sit for about 20 minutes. When you vacuum up the baking soda, the smells and some of the fine dirt go with it.

Chapter 4

Window-Cleaning Wisdom

If you can, clean on an overcast day. Windows won't streak as easily when the sun isn't shining, simply because you have plenty of time to wipe the fluid off before heat dries and streaks it on the spot. If you can't avoid washing windows on a sunny day, try to stay on the side of the house that's opposite the sun.

＊

Depend on dishwashing liquid for clean windows. You don't need to buy anything special, says Carla Edelen of Complete Cleaning, LLC, a janitorial service in St. Louis. "Just put a couple of squirts of dishwashing liquid in a bucket of water and use that." If you're the type who must have precise measurements, try 2 teaspoons (10 ml) of dishwashing soap per 5 gallons (19 L) of water.

＊

In the winter, add rubbing alcohol to the mix. "That's what we've found keeps the fluid from freezing on cold windows," says Carla Edelen. "I'd add about a quarter cup (60 ml) per gallon (3.8 L) of cleaning water."

＊

Head for the automotive department. If you do buy a commercial product, the automotive department is the way to go. The gallon-size windshield-washer fluid is cheaper, will fill several spray bottles, and doesn't streak easily at all.

Shift Gears

What will you use to wipe up that glass-cleaning fluid? The right answer can save you time and prevent streaks and future dust buildup:

- Newspaper is often touted as the best material for wiping windows. While it does prevent streaks, it's not really all that absorbent, and some modern inks run if you don't let the paper cure for a few days.

- Paper towels are okay, but they make a lot of static. Rubbing a paper towel back and forth across the window creates a static charge on the window, which attracts dust.

- Windows that are dried with a squeegee stay clean longer.

- Low-lint or lint-free cloths are another good choice. Options include cloth diapers or the type of tight-knit (not terry cloth) towels you can find in the auto aisle at the discount department store.

- In a pinch, paper coffee filters are more absorbent than newspaper and leave less static than paper towels.

＊

Try some H_2O. For lighter jobs, such as a few windows that aren't very dirty, plain lukewarm water will work. Aside from the price being right, it doesn't leave streaks on a warm day.

＊

Use white vinegar. Brighten up indoor windows with a clean, lint-free cloth that you've dipped in undiluted white vinegar. Rub until the dirt and the vinegar come off.

Make your own glass-cleaning quick wipes. To save time the next ten or twenty times you want to quickly wipe off a not-too-dirty window, spend a few minutes making some homemade glass wipes. Fold about thirty heavy-duty paper towels into fourths and stack them in an empty plastic baby-wipe box or similar-size disposable plastic food container, such as Gladware, with about a 3-cup (710 ml) capacity. Mix 2 tablespoons (30 ml) of rubbing alcohol, 1 teaspoon (5 ml) of white vinegar, and 3/4 cup (175 ml) of water, and pour the mix over the paper towels. Seal the container and let the paper towels absorb the liquid for at least four hours before using. This is a pretty inexact science due to the varying absorption abilities of different paper towels, so add more liquid or add more paper towels if the wipes aren't the right degree of "wet" after soaking. If the box starts to dry out before you've used all your quick wipes, just add a bit more water or cleaning solution and let it sit overnight again before using.

Once-a-Year Wonders

You can't clean *all* your windows in 10 minutes, but it's reasonable to expect each window to take about that long if you're organized, have a stepladder handy, and follow these steps:

1. **Use a bucket of suds and a sponge or cloth, not a spray bottle, for grimy windows.** If your windows have been hiding behind curtains or up in the attic attracting grime, you'll need more than a little spray bottle of Windex to clean them up in 10 minutes.

2. **Start by cleaning the windowsills and frames.** If you do it at the end, you'll just get the windowpanes dirty again. Vacuum the sills and edges of the frame, followed by running a dust cloth over the edges. Then, unless it's a surface that won't tolerate it, like unprotected wood, wipe the sills and frames with a damp cloth.

3. **Line the sills with newspaper or clean (but worn) towels.** Here's where those old papers come in handy—they'll catch any excess water, and you can just toss them later.

4. **If it's a really grimy job, wipe the glass with a damp cloth first.** That should take care of the very worst dirt, and you won't have to refresh the cleaning solution as often later in the process.

5. **Dip your sponge or cloth in the soapy water.** Then sponge the soap on an individual pane of glass in a back-and-forth motion to scrub loose any sediment. Wring the sponge out in the bucket before moving on to a new windowpane.

6. **Swipe the surface with the squeegee.** Pull the squeegee down the pane smoothly, and dry the squeegee blade after each swipe. Repeat until there's no more washer fluid on the window and the window is clean.

7. **Stick your index finger into a clean, dry cloth.** Then run your cloth-covered finger down each side of the window and across the bottom to clean and dry the edges, switching spots on the cloth as it gets soiled.

Sticky spots need special care. If a spot hasn't budged when you've finished washing, try scraping it off ever so gently with a craft knife (such as an X-Acto) or straight-edged razor. Test an inconspicuous area of the window first to make sure it won't scratch easily. Then spritz a bit of clear water on the spot and scrape. Or try very fine steel wool instead of the knife or razor.

Keep glass spot-free. Use one of those "rain shield" solutions such as Rain-X to keep newly cleaned outside windows from spotting. Purchase it at an automotive store, and apply it the same way you would on windshield glass.

Use a squeegee. Squeegee the insides of your windows from top to bottom, and the outsides from side to side. That way, if there's a streak, you can see which side needs another pass with the cleaning fluid.

Time-Saving Supplies

Buy a high-quality squeegee. Whether you order it online from a cleaning supply house or get one from an auto supply store, invest in a high-quality squeegee that won't miss any window-washing fluid and will last for a lot of windows (even the ones on your car!). It should have a very soft rubber blade without nicks or blemishes and will cost about $10. If you're into it, buy extra rubber blades at the same time so you'll have a replacement when your current blade wears out.

*

Go for the hose. Forget the ladder, use Windex Outdoor Window & Surface Cleaner. Wade Slate of Knoxville, Tennessee, likes Windex Outdoor so much for outdoor windows, particularly those on the second floor, that he says he wishes you could somehow use it for high indoor windows. "It comes in a special package that attaches to your garden hose, and then you can spray it on windows as far as your hose sprays," says Wade, who runs a lawn-care business and also branches out into pressure washing for about thirty customers annually. "It does a really good job and requires no rinsing. Of course, it leaves a few spots and you can't direct the spray perfectly from down below, but it looks much better than most people could do trying to hand-wash while standing on a ladder, and it takes much less time."

✳

Take down your screens. If the screens are up when you're washing windows, take them down. Make sure to wash the grooves where the screen frames rest with sudsy water and a cloth-wrapped screwdriver to scrape out the grime. Use masking tape to write a number on each window or door frame and put the same number on its screen, along with a zipper-locked sandwich bag containing any screws and bolts needed to replace the screen. That saves time when you want to put the clean screens back in place. Place the screens on newspapers, in the garage or outdoors, and use a household brush (like the kind you'd use to scrub the floor) to brush loose dirt and dust from both sides, or vacuum it off.

✳

Wash screens outside. If you want to wash a screen, wait until you can do it outdoors with a hose. Otherwise, you'll spend more time cleaning the floors and tub than you do washing the screens! Line your work space with plenty of newspapers and fill a pail with hot, soapy water. Use about 1/4 cup (60 ml) of liquid dishwashing detergent to 2 gallons (7.6 L) of water. Lean the screen against a wall, railing, porch, or tree. Dip a stiff brush (the kind you'd use to scrub floors) into the water and scrub both sides of the screen mesh. Then wipe the outer frame on both sides with a soft cloth dipped in the same soapy water. Use a fine spray of water from the hose to rinse and let the screens air-dry before replacing.

Chapter 5

Dealing with Dust, Mildew, and Other Allergens

Dust the television with a sheet of fabric softener. The static guard will keep dust from resettling. If anyone in the house is sensitive to perfumes, make sure to buy sheets without scent.

✳

To keep mini-blinds clean, dust them weekly with a lamb's-wool duster. Make sure to close the blinds first, and remember that both sides get dirty and require dusting. A lamb's-wool duster is also good for lampshades because it attracts dirt and won't leave a residue the way a rag might.

Once-a-Year Wonders

Take out and towel-dry mini-blinds. If you really want mini-blinds to get clean, follow these steps: Take them all the way out of their frames. Then take them outside and set them on the pavement or in a small wading pool, and wash them with a few drops of dishwashing liquid in warm water. Follow that with a rinse of clean water. It will take just 10 minutes for each blind.

*

Dance while you dust. Get dust up and out of the room on laundry day and get motivated at the same time, says Shawn Simpson, a former office manager for a group of psychotherapists, who lives in Belfair, Washington. "I put old, but clean, tube socks over my hands and arms and put an Aretha Franklin record on, cranked up loud, in the background. I let the music take me anywhere to dust anything. When the socks get dirty on one side, I take 'em off and put 'em back on inside out and go again 'til they get dirty again or I am danced out, and then they go directly into the wash." Shawn's favorite tune to dust by? "Freeway of Love."

＊

Pick up some dust on your way to the laundry. Cathy Steever, a working-and-commuting mother of four, makes the most of time spent loading laundry. "Since I have to wash it anyway, I use a dirty sock to wipe off the top of the washer and dryer, which really seem to attract dust and lint," says Cathy, who lives in Medfield, Massachusetts, outside Boston. "Then I clean off the soap buildup—or whatever that stuff is that builds up in the dispensers in the washer—right before I run a load of laundry, and then toss in the dirty sock and wash it with the rest of the load."

Shift Gears

Put that feather duster down. Sure, they look cute with a French maid's costume, but feather dusters just stir up dust and cause it to settle somewhere else. The same goes for the dry paintbrushes that you'll often see recommended for dabbing dust out of tight spots. Instead, use a cloth with dusting spray or a piece of flannel—anything that will actually remove the dust to another surface where you can dispose of it instead of shooting particles into the air. If you need to dust hard-to-reach spots, use cotton swabs for small spaces, and a dusting cloth or sock draped over a mop handle for corners and underneath heavy furniture.

✳

Save yourself some soot with salt. Toss 1/2 cup (100 g) of salt on your fireplace logs (just the real kind) every two weeks to reduce soot formation in the fireplace.

Change the vacuum bag to sweep out bacteria. "The major cause of odors in vacuum cleaners is from bacteria growing in the bag," says Georgia Jones, owner of the online retail store Vacuum Cleaner Bags . . . and More. "Change it at least once a month—more often is better if you have pets. The whole reason you use the vacuum is to remove dirt and germs from your house, so toss the bag and *really* get it out of your house!" If you're conscientious about changing the bag, you'll prolong the life of the vacuum, too. "A clogged-up bag also causes your motor to run hotter, causing strain and reducing the motor's life. The few cents you save in bags can be quickly lost on the dollars that you'll spend for motor repairs." When you buy a vacuum, opt for a model with bags you can buy readily at the grocery store or at a discount department store.

10 Minutes of Prevention

Keep dogs out of the bedroom with a baby gate. Breathing in cat or dog hair all night and lying on bedding that has their saliva and dander are surefire triggers for allergies, so do your best to keep animals out of the bedroom. A deadbolt is all that will work for cats, but a baby gate is usually sufficient for dogs.

$*$

Give pets their own human-scented sleeping arrangements. "Cats and dogs aren't trying to thwart you by sleeping where you sleep or on your clothes," explains Tom Russell, a longtime pet owner and graduate of several dog-training classes in Knoxville, Tennessee. "They just really like things that smell like their owners. To keep them from getting hair and saliva, which is what most people are allergic to, all over your stuff, give them their own things that smell like you. Sleep with their new bed pillow or blanket for a few days before you place it out for them, for example, or set it in with the dirty laundry or your shoes for a while."

*

Roll tape over cat hair on the couch. With fourteen beloved felines and an allergy, Jim Slate's wife, Liz, "tends to sneeze a lot," he says. But they do what they can to keep cat hairs off the couch with a roll of thick masking tape, the kind people use to tape windows before painting. "We reverse the tape so the sticky side is out, wrapping it all the way around the outside of the tape roll," says the Winnsboro, South Carolina, resident. "Then we roll it over the couch or the upholstery in the car, and the hair really sticks to it. When it won't pick up any more, we tear off the exposed piece and reverse a new piece."

Eliminate cat urine odors with orange. Jim Slate and his wife, Liz, live on a lake in the South Carolina countryside, and homeless cats just seem to find their way to the place. Kitties like Champion, who went from being an orange-and-white scrap of stray to considering himself boss of the house (and thirteen other cats) in just two weeks, mean that the Slates contend with lots of allergy-inducing cat urine—both from intentional spraying and cats missing the litter box. "We've found that an off-the-shelf orange cleaner, like 409 Orange Power, works better than the stuff that's specially designed to deodorize cat urine," says Jim. "It costs about half as much, but it covers the odor well enough that other cats aren't drawn to the same spot to do their worst."

Try a 3M Filtrete forced-air furnace filter first. Before you invest in a portable air purifier, consider an inexpensive filter for forced-air furnaces and air conditioners, says ConsumerSearch, a Web-based publishing company in New York and Washington, D.C., that "reviews the reviews" to help consumers find products that are top-rated or best bets in their class. The reviews they evaluated say that the 3M Filtrete, readily available at popular discount department stores, "is very good at removing the most common allergens, like dust and pet dander. They don't do as well with smoke, and aren't effective with odors. Still, a $15 filter, replaced four times a year, may improve your indoor air quality enough that you don't need a more expensive portable unit at all." In addition to the hundreds of dollars that an air purifier costs to purchase, consider that filter replacements for the unit may be as much as $40 or $50 each, and units with electrostatic plates produce ozone, often at unacceptable levels.

*

Move your houseplants so they don't sit directly on a carpet or rug.
Set them on a plastic or clay saucer, preferably on linoleum or hard
wood that's easy to wipe clean. Even better, place the saucers on a small
platform with rollers so you can just roll them a few feet when you
need to clean. Otherwise, excess moisture from overwatering or simple
condensation will form mildew on the carpet, which is hard to clean
and a powerful irritant to allergy sufferers.

10 Minutes of Prevention

Salt away mildew on plastic shower curtains. Soak a new plastic shower
curtain for 24 hours in 1 gallon (3.8 L) of warm water mixed with 1 cup
(200 g) of salt before hanging it. That will cut down on mildew for months.

Use vinegar to combat smoke. Of course, no one should be smoking indoors, but placing a few small bowls of vinegar throughout the house will absorb smoke odors from a wood-burning stove or fireplace. Another option: Dampen a dish towel with full-strength vinegar and wave it around the room. Or place a shallow pan of baking soda inside the fireplace after you clean it to absorb soot odors.

Damp ashes so they stay down. Use a plastic spray bottle filled with clean water to spritz the ashes in the bottom of the fireplace before sweeping them up—damp ashes won't go airborne on you. Just don't overdo it, because wet ashes are a headache to clean up.

Scatter baking powder to get rid of smoke smells on upholstery. Leave it for a few hours and then vacuum it up. Don't forget the spaces under the cushions!

＊

Nuke nicotine stains on walls with Simple Green. Wash the wall with full-strength Simple Green (available in gallon-size containers at most dollar stores) and a sponge. Test an unobtrusive spot first, and make sure to rinse the sponge thoroughly in a separate bucket of hot, clean water as you go along. Follow through with a rinse of clear water on a slightly damp sponge, then let the walls air-dry.

＊

Wash smoke from clothes by adding baking soda to the wash.
Add 1/4 cup (55 g) of baking soda to a load of laundry and cut the detergent by a third to clean smoke from clothing. Best of all, if you're allergic to laundry soap perfumes, baking soda tends to be hypoallergenic and still makes clothes smell good.

Chapter 6

Let There Be (Clean) Lights

Skip the cleaning solution on lightbulbs. Instead, wipe them clean with a lint-free, untreated towel. If you've gone too long before cleaning and the bulb has some resistant buildup, try a cloth barely dampened with plain water and follow through quickly by drying it off with a clean cloth. Fluorescent tubes also come clean with a barely damp cloth, and you can clean recessed can lights with a damp cloth and then hand-dry them with a lint-free cloth. Make sure you take this simple step often because dirt keeps bulbs from delivering the most light for your dollar, and after a while next to all that warmth, it can start to cast a musty smell about the room.

Time-Saving Supplies

Save steps, and mess, with long-life lightbulbs. It's such a big production to change lightbulbs: Finding the stepladder, disposing of the delicate used bulb, listening to all those jokes. Matt Herd believes you should go through the hassle only every seven years. "Any of those super-long-life bulbs are going to save you time and energy," says Matt, who is head of both the lighting and electrical departments at a hardware superstore in Topeka, Kansas. "There are also compact fluorescent bulbs now that you can put in place of a common lightbulb, and they'll last up to seven years. They're great, as long as you don't need to dim the light in that room or from that lamp."

✳

Let chandeliers drip-dry-and clean. Matt Herd, head of both the lighting and electrical departments at a hardware superstore in Topeka, Kansas, recommends commercial chandelier-cleaning products if you want to minimize the time you spend washing—and on a stepladder. "You protect the surface below it with lots of newspapers, then step on a ladder and soak the chandelier down with the sprayer," he says. "All the mess literally just drips off—no rinsing or washing." The product Matt is most familiar with is made by Angelo, but other brands are also available, he says.

✳

If you have pleated lampshades, buy a baby hairbrush. Take the lampshade outside and brush the pleats from top to bottom. The soft bristles will remove dust from the narrow crevices between pleats without crushing the shape of the lampshade.

＊

Mary had a little lampshade duster in the making. Purchase a lamb's wool duster, which has built-in lanolin, to dust paper, fabric, or fine silk lampshades.

＊

Give glass shades a bath. Wash glass lampshades in a plastic tub filled with soapy water, using dishwashing liquid or mild laundry detergent. First, though, put a towel on the bottom to keep the globes from bumping each other or getting scratched by the plastic. When they've soaked clean (with a little help from your hand and a soft, soapy rag if needed), rinse them thoroughly and let them drain dry on a doubled-over bath towel.

10 Minutes of Prevention

Enjoy candlelight with less muss and fuss using these tactics:

- Buy beeswax tapers: They're smokeless, and their higher cost is offset by the fact that they burn longer than paraffin.

- It may seem frou-frou, but putting a candle out with a snuffer instead of blowing keeps wax from getting all over the table or on the floor. You may have to seek out a pewter or candle store to find one, or order one online. Antiques stores also often have decorative snuffers.

- Bobeches, small transparent drip dishes that you slip around the base of tapers, will keep candles from dripping wax on the table or on hard-to-clean candlesticks. They're available at candle and craft stores and some home boutiques—or order a supply online.

＊

Take aim at switch-plate grime. Get the grime—not the surrounding wall—when you're cleaning a light-switch plate. Take an extra 10 minutes to cut a cardboard frame to put around the light-switch plate before you clean it. That will keep cleaning solution off your precious wall or wallpaper.

＊

Scrub those plates. Use a mild all-purpose cleanser, such as vinegar and water, to clean plastic light-switch plates. Since they attract so many grimy fingerprints, though, you might need the increased power of a degreasing cleaner such as 409. Or put a dab of rubbing alcohol on the corner of a soft rag and try to rub out the fingerprints with your finger. In any case, finish up by rinsing with plain water and drying with a clean cloth.

Proceed with Caution

Never use pine oil cleaners on light-switch plates. Despite your best efforts, the cleaner might get on the wall, and pine can damage painted surfaces.

Part Three

Inside and Out

Chapter 7

Livable Living Rooms, Functional Family Rooms

Chill out before you dust. Before you dust the coffee table and knick-knacks, turn on the AC. The filter from the air conditioner will get rid of the dust that ends up in the air instead of on the dust cloth.

✳

Pick up before you suck up. Before you vacuum, pick up all the pins, tacks, nails, and, yes, socks with your hands or even a magnet. Then you don't have to stop every time the vacuum catches on such an item, or go back and sort through the bag or bagless insert to retrieve Junior's soccer sock.

Shift Gears

Vacuum first, dust afterward. Don't waste time dusting before you vacuum. Often, the vacuum kicks dust back into the air where it will soon settle on your clean furniture. Therefore, you can save yourself time and frustration by dusting afterward.

✳

Use a whisk broom. Whisk brooms are ideal for hard-to-reach corners and around the baseboards. Whisk before you vacuum, and you can just pick up the debris with the upright or an attachment.

✳

Don't forget the windowsills. If you habitually open the windows for a good breeze in the living room or den, just as habitually dust and wash the sills. Not only does all that opening and closing attract grimy fingerprints, but dust that comes to rest on the sill will get blown into the room to stick to lampshades, knickknacks, and the like.

✳

When you run out of Pledge or Endust, try a homemade concoction. Stir 1 tablespoon (15 ml) of high-quality olive oil into 2 tablespoons (30 ml) of lemon juice or white vinegar and you're on your way: Spray it from a plastic spray bottle or dip a clean, soft cloth in the mixture to clean and polish wood furniture. The vinegar extracts dirt from the wood and the oil keeps it from drying out as a result of your efforts.

Look for liquid jojoba.

If you actually prefer to make homemade furniture cleaner and polish and have a couple of extra minutes when you shop, invest in some liquid wax jojoba. You can find the stuff at most health food stores. Use it in place of the oil in the furniture cleaner/polish—it never goes rancid, in the cabinet or on your tables and shelves.

Clean and Green

Try an herbalist or an Internet retailer for pure sources of lemon oil for cleaning and polish. Lemon oil is the perfect product for wood polishing because it restores luster and acts as an antiseptic. But most commercial products are not entirely natural, and they may contain petroleum distillates. To make a natural furniture polish that smells great, whip together 10 drops of pure lemon oil and 2 tablespoons (30 ml) of lemon juice, then stir in 5 drops of high-quality olive oil or jojoba. Apply just a bit on a soft piece of clean flannel, then rub the furniture to a fine luster.

*

Clean a glass clock face with rubbing alcohol.

Dip a soft rag into a bit of alcohol, and rub the glass until the alcohol—and the grime—is gone.

*

Keep DVDs dust-free.

Strange as it seems, you should keep your DVD collection at a distance from the TV. The static from the television is a dust magnet, and it will get all over the plastic cases of the DVDs. Instead, consider storing DVDs in a closed archival-quality photo box across the room from the TV.

10 Minutes of Prevention

If you're tired of dusting stuff, try these ways to cut back on knickknacks and clutter:

✔ To reduce your CD and DVD collection, take a stroll through a used music or movie store. When you see the prices discards are drawing, you might be inspired to clean out your own hoard and get some cash.

✔ Donate where the stuff will be appreciated. Steve Little, a longtime librarian in Chattanooga, Tennessee, reminds us that while a lot of books aren't appropriate for a public library collection, most public libraries will happily accept donations of videotapes, audiobooks, CDs, and DVDs, as long as they're in good shape. And, if you start checking out music and DVDs from the library instead of purchasing them, you can quickly cut down on what you have to clean.

✔ Remember this when you're at the mall. All Joan Kennedy does to reduce the knickknacks at her vintage 1910 dwelling in Hampton, Virginia, is to calculate how much cleaning and maintenance they'll require—while she's still at the store. "The end result is I just don't buy them," she says.

- ✔ Don't let knickknacks sneak in. Joan, who is an architect by training, also recommends planning a room design with one or two nice things, such as a large piece of pottery or a bowl, and then banning all others, even (or especially!) if they're gifts.

- ✔ Purge the magazines. Even though she's a professional magazine journalist and writing coach, Dorothy Foltz-Gray of Knoxville, Tennessee, limits herself to three issues of any magazine title, giving the others away to the library or recycling them.

Dust your books. Wipe lightly with an untreated, soft flannel or microfiber cloth to dust books. Dusting spray or polish tends to just smear the dust around, as does pressing too firmly.

*

Give books breathing room. Even though it seems like it's saving space, don't double-shelve books. To keep books from mildewing and molding, provide air circulation above and behind them. This means just one row of books per shelf, and an inch or so between the top of the books and the underside of the shelf above. This approach makes it easier to dust the books and shelves, too.

*

Dust—but don't clean-oil paintings. You can dust oil paintings, but let professionals handle any necessary cleaning. Otherwise, you'll most likely ruin your art.

Proceed with Caution

Be careful when cleaning framed art and photographs. Never spray cleanser or water onto the frame. The liquid can seep behind the glass and damage the pictures. Instead, lightly wet a clean cloth to wipe the frame and glass. If it takes just an extra minute or two, take smaller mirrors and frames off the wall to clean them, which greatly reduces the chance of accidentally getting cleaning fluid on the frames when you're working at arm's length, and also gives you a chance to wipe off the wall behind them.

*

Don't use a feather duster to clean houseplants. "It's the easiest way to spread tiny pests like spider mites or mealybugs," says Barbara Pleasant, a longtime garden writer in Pisgah Forest, North Carolina, and author of *The Complete Houseplant Survival Manual*. But houseplants do need some attention, since they can't absorb CO_2 and light through a layer of dust (and dead leaves look bad and get all over the floor!). "Clean the leaves of large-leafed plants like sheffelera or philodendrons by hand with a soft cloth or sponge dipped in soapy water, and you'll remove any pests in the process," says Barbara. Ferns and other houseplants with fine foliage have to go offsite for cleaning, because you'll need to spray them with a fine spray of water. "In summer, you can do this outdoors, but in winter it's best to set plants in the bathtub and work them over with room-temperature water from a pump spray bottle," she says.

＊

Clean plastic kiddie furniture and big plastic toys very gently. Don't use an abrasive such as scouring powder, or even one of those green scrub pads, because plastic scratches easily. Instead, wash it down with a soft cloth and a solution of one capful of Ivory liquid dishwashing detergent per gallon (3.8 L) of water, then wipe back over it with a damp cloth and dry.

＊

Clean small plastic toys in the dishwasher. Everything from Happy Meal giveaways and plastic rattles to Fisher Price and Playmobil figurines can go through the dishwasher in a mesh bag or the silver-ware basket. Just as you would with plastic glasses, rub a little baking soda on any gunk that looks like it might be stubborn before loading the washer.

*

Color scratches away. Look no further than the kids' crayon box if you've got tiny scratches on finished wood furniture. Spend some time matching the color and then run the crayon across the scratch and scrape the excess with a matchbook cover or a credit card. Rub in a little furniture polish or lemon oil afterward. If you've got the time and energy and want a really close match, you can purchase furniture crayons at most home stores. The application process is about the same.

*

Tackle tough stains like a Tartar. Check out the baking aisle if your plastic furniture or toys have tough stains. Cream of tartar is sold alongside the flour and sugar, probably near the baking powder and cornstarch. Mix 1 tablespoon (9 g) of it with 1 tablespoon (15 ml) of lemon juice or white vinegar, and rub the paste on the stain with a cotton swab. Leave it on there for half an hour, then wipe it off, and the stain should be much lighter, if not entirely bleached out.

*

Take off the cushions every time you tackle the couch. That's where all the grime, sand, and, happily, pocket change, settles. Make sure to brush the cushions with a whisk broom or the upholstery attachment of the vacuum. Do the same for the dirt beneath the cushions.

*

Let your couch covers go to the dogs. If your dogs will inevitably be perching on the couch, go with the flow, says Susan Castle of Chattanooga, Tennessee. An experienced retail housewares buyer who used to own a lamp boutique, Susan is also the proud owner of three dachshunds. Instead of fighting it, she buys machine-washable coverlets and keeps them on the couch and chairs that the dogs favor. "Heavy-duty tablecloths work best for me. You can buy them at the department store in the linen department," she says. "That seems to be the best way to find something that looks good and matches the living room." Washable fleece throws are another good bet, she says, because the dogs really like them, and you can whip them off and toss them in the washer if allergy-prone humans are going to sit on the same settee where the dogs have been.

*

Have some fresh air with your fire. Open a window a couple of inches when you're burning a fire to keep the room from getting smoky. The air from the window will go up the chimney. Test to make sure by lighting a match, blowing it out, and watching where the smoke goes.

*

Keep soot off your carpets with a fireplace rug. Purchase a nonflammable rug from a fireplace supply store. Keep it on the hearth or in front of the fireplace, and sparks won't create ugly, dirty marks on the carpet.

*

Use a chimney cap. A cap will prevent water damage and keep squirrels, chimney swifts, and the like from nesting in the chimney. A chimney cap also keeps debris from blocking the chimney and inviting carbon monoxide into the house.

*

Labs (and other dogs) love leather. Next time you purchase a couch, go with leather if you have dogs. Joan Kennedy, who owns both a vintage home and two teenaged Westies in Hampton, Virginia, is almost fanatical about having a leather couch. "It is great for anyone with allergies," she says. "Unlike fabric couches, the leather couches don't absorb dog smells. And they're easy to clean. You just wipe it down with a cloth that's just damp enough to pick up dirt and dog hair, and follow it with a quick swipe with a dry cloth."

*

Clean woodstove and fireplace doors. Clean tough gunk from the glass doors on woodstoves and fireplaces by scraping off deposits (careful!) with a razor blade or craft knife. Make sure the doors are cool first. Then proceed with the lesser stains by sponging them with a mix of 1 gallon (3.8 L) of water and 1 cup (235 ml) of white vinegar. Wipe it away with a lint-free paper towel or cloth. You can also purchase a commercial fireplace glass cleaner at a fireplace store, but you'll probably still need to scrape the gunk with a razor blade if you've gone a while between cleanings.

*

Clean a slate hearth with plain hot water and a dry cloth.

Then wipe it down with lemon oil and a soft cloth to make it shine.
If the cloth comes away dirty, rub off the dirt that the water didn't pick
up with lemon oil, and then apply a second coat for shine.

Once-a-Year Wonders

If you've lived in your home more than a year or so, wash the living room or
family room walls when you can, particularly if you have a wood or gas fireplace. Take it one wall at a time, and once you have the supplies assembled
and everything off the wall, it will take only 10 minutes. Even if you can't see
the difference, you'll be washing out a lot of oil and grime. This will freshen
the air and just make the whole place feel better. Here's how to proceed:

1. Be sure to pull any furniture well away from the wall in question and
   cover it with newspapers or an old sheet.

2. Take the picture frames and posters off the wall, but leave the nails up: just impale a small piece of sponge on them to protect your hand from gashes.

3. Mix up a wall-washing solution with 1 gallon (3.8 L) of warm water, 1/4 cup (55 g) washing soda (the Arm & Hammer type is usually right next to the laundry detergent at the store), 1/4 cup (60 ml) white vinegar, and 1/2 cup (120 ml) ammonia.

4. Dip a natural sponge in the mixture and then wipe the wall from the bottom up, wringing the sponge in the ammonia mixture every few swipes and refreshing the solution when it starts to look like tea.

5. Find a friend or one of the kids to hold the stepladder if you need it to reach the high spots, but leave the bucket on the floor and head up the ladder rungs with just the sponge.

*

"Dust" lightweight curtains in the clothes dryer. Run them through on a no-heat cycle for 10 or 15 minutes and the lint trap should remove most of the dust.

*

Vacuum dust from heavy drapes with the soft brush attachment. To keep the suction from drawing in the drapes instead of the dust, wrap a pantyhose foot over the end of the nozzle.

*

Dampen your drapes. For a quick pick-me-up for velvet drapes, dip a chamois cloth in hot water. Wring it out thoroughly and gently brush it down the curtains.

Chapter 8

A Cleaner Kitchen

Wipe counters with a damp, not wet, cloth. Too much water left on the counter will spot and can even cause mildew or harbor bacteria. To make sure your countertop dries quickly and completely without resorting to a towel, wring the cloth you're wiping with very well. A good rule of thumb is that the cloth should be about as damp as clothes just coming out of the laundry spin cycle. In fact, that's a good time to wipe down the counters—just as your dishcloths come out of the wash.

＊

Use foam cleaners on upright refrigerator exteriors. The foam clings on and gives the stuff a few minutes to work at breaking down dirt and grime before sliding down the side.

＊

Clean vinyl chairs regularly. To keep body oil from hardening vinyl on kitchen chairs and making it crack, clean them often. Rub off the oil itself (usually where your neck hits the chair and on the armrests) with a damp sponge sprinkled with baking soda. Wash the rest with a weak solution of water and dishwashing liquid: Dishwashing detergents made to cut grease are ideal, but use just a drop or two per gallon (3.8 L) of hot water.

✳

Wipe crumbs from the table into your hand, not onto the floor.

While it's easier to wipe debris from the kitchen table onto the floor so you can deal with it later, too often later never comes—and it's harder to bend down to get stuff up off the floor than to just put crumbs in the trash in the first place. Wipe tables and counters with a barely damp rag and cup it to push debris into your other hand, positioned just below the flat surface. If you're too squeamish to touch unknown particles from the counter, use a small dustpan to catch the crumbs.

Proceed with Caution

Kitchen appliances and surfaces take a lot of abuse. Don't make matters worse by using the wrong cleaners.

- **Use dishwasher detergent in the dishwasher**. Dishwashing liquid is a great all-purpose cleaner, but dishwashing detergents (like Cascade) are meant to be used in dishwashers only. According to the Soap and Detergent Association, based in Washington, D.C., you shouldn't use it for sinks, windows, floors, or clothing, mostly because it's formulated just to do a great job on dishes, but also because it may damage some other surfaces.

- **Don't use orange cleaners around kitchen appliances.** Those handy orange cleaners may contain petroleum distillates, which break down the rubber gaskets around refrigerators and dishwashers. Instead, use a spray bottle half full of water and a squirt of Ivory liquid as the basic all-purpose surface cleaner in the kitchen, and wipe it off with a clean, soft towel or paper towels.

Use Ivory liquid on marble countertops. And make sure you dry the counter directly afterward so you don't have water spots. Anything harsher, particularly the acid in vinegar- or orange-based cleaners, will damage the surface.

Baby granite countertops. Granite is popular for floors and countertops because it's so hard and durable, but it can't hack harsh cleaners. Make sure you wipe it down with only lukewarm water or a commercial granite cleaner, or the surface will get dingy, maybe irreversibly so.

Check the label before using commercial cleaners on ceramic tile. You can clean a ceramic tile countertop with just about anything, from 409 to vinegar, but check the product label first to be on the safe side. Better safe than sorry!

Be extra-careful when cleaning wood surfaces. Don't use steel wool, scrub brushes, or any other item that can scratch the wood to wipe kitchen cabinets and other wood surfaces. Anytime you use an all-purpose household cleaner, read the label carefully to make sure it won't ruin your finish, and even then test it on a hidden spot first.

✳

Keep a spray bottle filled with rubbing alcohol for spritzing stains.
Spray, then wipe the stains with a paper towel or clean cloth before they
set, says Louise Kurzeka, who with Pam Hix co-owns Everything's
Together, an organizing business in the Minneapolis area that sometimes
veers into cleaning if it affects household productivity.

✳

Use a bigger bowl. Here's a common sense tip: As a rule, use a bowl
that's too big when mixing ingredients and use a big pot when cooking.
This will prevent splatters and messes.

✳

When you defrost a chest freezer, use a clean mop to swab the bottom.
When you've mopped up the defrosted water, keep the freezer smelling
fresh by mopping again with a solution of 1/4 cup (55 g) baking soda
dissolved in 1 gallon (3.8 L) of room-temperature water.

Reserve the self-cleaning oven feature for "big cleans," and use baking soda for spot checks. If you own a self-cleaning oven, it's just not worth the energy or the hours to rev it up every time a pot pie spills over. To keep the oven nice between cleanings, use baking soda and be patient. Sprinkle about 1/4 inch (6.25 mm) of baking soda over the mess (or the whole bottom of the oven if it needs it), and then dampen the baking soda with water from a spray bottle. Leave it alone for several hours, then dampen it again. Dampen it once more before bed, and scoop the baking soda, and the mess, out of the oven with a damp sponge when you wake up. Then rinse out the white residue with a little water-diluted vinegar on a paper towel.

If you clean the oven with commercial cleaner, bake some orange peels. Two or three orange peels baked in a 350°F (180°C, or gas mark 4) oven for about half an hour will get rid of that lingering oven-cleaner odor, says Jill Kendall Williams, an experienced caterer who lives in Knoxville, Tennessee.

*

Clean underneath large appliances, too. Stretch a dress sock over a yardstick and run it under the stove or fridge to pick up dust bunnies and lint.

10 Minutes of Prevention

It's much easier to prevent bacterial growth in the first place then to have to resort to harsh chemicals or tough scrubbing to get rid of it later. Here's how:

✓ Store hand and dish towels separately. That way, you don't have to worry about passing the bacteria from your hands to clean dishes.

✓ Bleach the cutting board. Spritz it with a solution of 1 teaspoon (5 ml) bleach per 1 quart (9464 ml) warm water once a week, then rinse with hot water, and you'll retard bacterial growth.

✓ Sterilize utensils with bleach. When you use forks, spoons, or knives to prepare raw meat, immediately dunk them in a container of warm water with a half teaspoon of bleach added.

*

Wash your fridge in increments. If the prospect of spending the day cleaning the refrigerator is repulsive, just clean one section at a time. Clear out the meat keeper, for example, or a single shelf. Sprinkle baking soda on a damp (not wet!) cloth or sponge, scrub that area's surfaces, and then wipe them dry with another cloth. Another day, try another spot.

*

Clean oven racks, not the whole oven. To at least nudge your grimy oven in the right direction, clean the racks—it's mostly a matter of waiting. Place the racks in a very large, heavy-duty plastic bag inside the bathtub or shower, and then fill the bag with very hot water to cover the racks. Add 1/4 cup (60 ml) of grease-cutting dishwashing liquid such as Dawn and 1 cup (235 ml) of white vinegar, swish them around, and tie or clip the bag shut. Let the racks soak for at least three hours. Take the sealed bag outside, open it, and remove the racks, hopefully leaving the grime behind in the water (which makes a great addition to the compost heap). Rinse the racks with the hose, or put them back in the shower and turn it on to rinse them. Dry them with a cloth.

✳

Clean a glass coffeepot or percolator with salt sprinkled on a lemon wedge. Run the lemon wedge over the coffee buildup, then rinse the pot with hot water and dry the inside with a clean cloth.

✳

Shine and degerm stainless-steel kitchen appliances with hand sanitizer. If you already buy it for school, the bathroom, or to use in a sick room, try some waterless hand sanitizer to clean and polish stainless-steel appliances—no rinsing required!

10 Minutes of Prevention

A little nonstick spray goes a long way toward making cleanup easier in the kitchen. See for yourself:

- Spray it on the slow-cooker insert before adding ingredients, and gunk wipes off easily after cooking.
- Spritzing the inside of plastic containers before you store tomato-based dishes like spaghetti with sauce saves you time and work trying to scrub off those greasy red stains.
- Spray a bit on the center shaft of the food processor to keep gooey foods like dough from sticking.
- When you're baking, line the pan with aluminum foil, and spray the foil with cooking spray.

To loosen debris in the food disposal, throw a couple of ice cubes down the hatch. Follow that with a couple of orange or lemon peels, if you have them, then flush with cold (never hot) water—citrus is a natural degreaser. Amy Witsil, a mechanical engineer by training who runs a household in Chapel Hill, North Carolina, combines the two ideas, freezing white vinegar (another natural degreaser) into cubes and then sending a couple through the garbage disposal.

Ban burnt popcorn smells. The smell of burnt popcorn is the worst! Take the odor out of the air by microwaving 1/2 cup (120 ml) of water with a tablespoon (15 ml) of vanilla or lemon extract long enough to heat it to boiling. Turn off the microwave, but leave the mixture inside for 12 hours or overnight. When you open up, all that should greet you is the scent of the extract, not eau de popcorn.

*

Skip those special microwave wipes. Amy Witsil of Chapel Hill, North Carolina, is a home-based worker, and she and her three kids use the microwave several times a day for lunch and snacks. It gets gross, but she doesn't see any need to buy those special wipes designed to heat up in the microwave for cleaning. "Even though my husband Matt and I are just forty, we're already in downsize mode, and I just can't think why you'd give over space to a product like that when you can just use a pie plate with an inch (2.5 cm) of half water and half white vinegar in the bottom. Heat it on high for three minutes, and the steam will loosen those tough, crusted stains and make it easier to wipe the inside down with paper towels or a clean cloth."

*

Let the blender clean itself. Even blenders that theoretically come apart to be washed in the dishwasher can just as easily, or maybe more easily, wash themselves, and it's definitely the best approach for the kind that doesn't come apart. Fill the still-assembled unit halfway with water, add a drop of dishwashing liquid and four ice cubes, and blend on the highest speed for one minute. Here's where another benefit comes in: Now you have a pitcher of soapy water to dump on soaking dishes or the houseplants. (A very diluted solution of soapy water like this kills houseplant pests without toxic chemicals.) Rinse the blender and set it upside down on a towel to dry.

*

Use rice to clean a coffee grinder. Run 1/2 cup (95 g) of dry rice through the grinder to clean and sharpen the blades. If you're not going to cook the rest, buy whatever's cheapest—the grinder won't know the difference.

Let the slow cooker cook its way to cleanliness. Pour soapy water (about the same strength as you use to hand-wash dishes) into your slow cooker and let it cook on high for at least an hour before rinsing.

Proceed with Caution

✔ **Never, ever immerse any electrical appliance in water.** That includes slow cookers, coffeemakers, toasters, coffee grinders, waffle irons, blenders, and electric skillets.

✔ **Never spray cleaning solution directly on an electrical appliance.** It could go awry and cause any number of combustible reactions. Instead, spray the cleaning solution (after reading the instructions to make sure it's appropriate) on a cloth, sponge, or paper towel, and use that to wipe the appliance.

✳

Always let a toaster oven cool before cleaning. Once it's cool, take the racks out and clean them in the sink with a nylon scrubber or a soapy scouring pad. Wipe down the outside with a gentle abrasive such as Soft Scrub or some baking soda on a sponge, wipe clean with a damp sponge, and dry to a fine polish. If the sides are plastic, clean them with watered-down liquid dishwashing soap or baking soda on a damp sponge. Clean out the crumb tray often or the toaster will catch on fire.

✳

Turn the toaster upside down to clean it. Holding the toaster over the garbage can, give it a good thump to dislodge loose crumbs (or remove and clean the crumb tray at the bottom if it's obvious how to proceed or you still have the manufacturer's instructions). Clean the outside by spraying some glass cleaner on a sponge and rubbing it gently until it shines. Plastic-sided toasters can be cleaned with a mild liquid dish-washing soap or baking soda and water.

Keep a stubborn stopper in your sink. If you do only one thing to improve the flow of dirty-to-clean dishes at your house, keep all the sink stoppers operative, even if you have to replace the pop-up type monthly or call a plumber in to adjust the other types. There's nothing worse than thinking you're soaking dishes in warm suds and coming back to see just a few bits of foam and a stack of dirty plates in the sink! And any dish that's been sitting for a while without benefit of soaking is going to take a long, long time to clean. Plus, a working stopper that can actually be loosened to let water drain while it catches debris will greatly diminish your odds of rotting leftovers in the bottom of the sink.

Shift Gears

Myths abound about how to have a clean kitchen. Try these truths:

- **No sponge is better than a dirty sponge.** Surprisingly, messy people can have healthier kitchens than neatniks, because they're less likely to wipe down a counter with a bacteria-laden sponge. Always sniff before wiping, and favor damp cotton cloths over sponges, because they're easier to drop in with the other laundry, and it's much more obvious when they're too dirty to use. If you literally do it everyday, you can keep a new or clean sponge clean by running it with the dishes in the dishwasher. Otherwise, give up on a stinky sponge and buy a new one, or switch to dishcloths.

- **You *can* run a half-full dishwasher.** Endless hours are wasted soaking dishes that have sat in the sink for days waiting for a berth in the dishwasher, or rewashing dishes that have developed a film in the washer from, say, a drip of milk left in the bottom or dried cheese. It's much more efficient to just go ahead and run dishes when you have half a load. Cut down the amount of soap you use and run a short cycle if you have it, but keep the dishes moving through and you'll save soap, water, and energy in the long run.

✓ **You *can* hand-wash dishes even if you have a washer.** As a corollary to the half-full dishwasher, it's also preferable to hand-wash, dry, and put away the few dishes that wouldn't fit in the load. If you wait for the next time there are enough dishes to make a full load, the sink will be unusable and the dishes will grow increasingly difficult to get clean with each passing hour.

✳

Keep swatches of newspaper on hand for clearing off plates. If people at your house seem to have a tough time clearing uneaten food off their dinner plates, or you always have a few icky baked beans sticking to the bottom of a pan, get out your scissors. Then cut a section of black-and-white newspaper into 6-inch (15-cm) squares to use as disposable "scrapers," and keep them ready and waiting near the trash can. This should really cut down on the gunk swimming in your dishwater or caked on unwashed dishes. Unlike a spoon or fork, it's perfectly okay if the food adheres to the newspaper, and it won't scratch fine finishes, either. Wait three days for the newsprint to cure before you use it, though, so it won't smudge your hands.

Time-Saving Supplies

Soak stainless silverware in some bubbly. If you can buy 2 liters of store-brand carbonated water inexpensively, keep it on hand for silverware that's been used and left out for a while, recommends Keith Anders, a retired Marine who's now a shift manager for the Mellow Mushroom restaurant in Knoxville, Tennessee. "That's what we use to soak silverware until we can get it in the dishwasher, and it starts dissolving everything from salad dressing to tomato sauce, without spotting the stainless steel," says Keith. In the home kitchen, pour the carbonated water into a loaf pan, and add a cup (235 ml) or so of boiling water for extra oomph.

*

Freeze steel-wool soap pads between jobs. To keep a pad from rusting or dripping its soap all over the sink, slip it into a resealable plastic sandwich bag right after using it, and stash it in the freezer until you need it again. When you take it out, warm water will thaw it right away.

✳

Concentrate on cleaning grease from cabinets. Grease is the main culprit when it comes to dirty cabinets, so mix one part mild laundry detergent that touts its grease-fighting ability with two parts warm water, dip a sponge in it, and wipe down the outsides of your cabinets and kitchen storage drawers. Put a little extra elbow grease into the areas around door and drawer handles, since sticky fingers are constantly leaving a little grime behind.

✳

Remove everything from cabinet shelves, then wipe with warm water. Plain old water is usually enough to do the trick. If not, sprinkle a little warm water on the shelf (or the honey, or whatever is sticking), followed by some baking soda. Let it sit for 20 minutes and then wipe it off with a damp cloth.

Use car wax for a beautiful shine. Wipe down the outside of wood cabinets or pantries with a very thin coat of car wax. Dry, then buff.

*

Wear gloves to wash with baking (or washing) soda.

Even though cleaning everything from stove burners to walls is easy and environmentally safe with baking or washing soda, it will dry out your hands. Consider wearing gloves when you use it, and sprinkle just a bit of talcum powder inside first, to make sure they don't stick to your hands or make your skin smell rubbery.

Clean and Green

Here's what environmentally conscious folks use to clean in the kitchen:

Use vinegar instead of a commercial spot-free rinse solution in the dishwasher. "Just fill up that little receptacle in your dishwasher with undiluted white vinegar, and it will keep your glassware from spotting and help your dishes come clean," says Jill Kendall Williams, an experienced caterer and Web producer for the Home and Garden Television Network in Knoxville, Tennessee. To keep dishes from spotting, says Jill, think like an astronaut. "Add a tablespoon of orange-flavored breakfast drink to your regular powdered detergent. Add the detergent to the washer first, then pour the breakfast drink on top and close the container."

A half-water, half-vinegar solution on a sponge cleans gunk off cabinet doors. For out-of-the-ordinary buildup, try undiluted vinegar or make a paste that's the consistency of yogurt out of baking soda and water.

*

Reorganize your shelves with ordinary boxes. Once you've taken everything out to clean your cabinet, you might as well make things easier for the next go-round. Your groceries will stay neater if you group them according to use. Put all the boxes of breakfast cereal in one larger box, for example, or all the envelopes of seasonings, from chili to salad dressings, in a shoe box you can flip through like an index card file. No need to use a lid unless you want to, but be sure to label each box so you know what you're pulling out when you need it.

*

Store stuff in plastic, not ceramic. Put baking ingredients and coffee in plastic containers or pitchers instead of ceramic canisters. That way you can put them out of sight in the cabinets, and the plastic keeps the stuff fresher, too.

*

File away flat items. Store baking sheets, trays, and cutting boards upright in a metal or plastic file box.

*

Rack up your aprons. Put a spare coat rack in the kitchen to hold aprons and oven mitts, instead of constantly trying to cram them into a too-shallow drawer or on a hook.

*

Skip the dish rack. Do away with that bulky dish-draining rack if you hand-wash dishes infrequently. Instead, use a clean bath towel on the rare occasions when you need to air-dry dishes.

*

Recycle plastic containers. You've heard it before and you'll hear it again, but mismatched plastic containers really do take a lot of space in the kitchen and they don't really aid your cause. Take some time to see which ones match and are used at least once a week. To feel better about discarding the rest, make sure you recycle them, or donate them to an animal shelter.

10 Minutes of Prevention

Make more space and prevent messes in the refrigerator and pantry with these time- and work-saving tips:

- Keep the name and hours of a food-pantry charity posted on the refrigerator, so you can cull dried and canned goods that the family doesn't like and give them away while they're still good for somebody.

- Limit how much fresh food spoils and makes a mess in your refrigerator by buying less. Just buy enough for a few meals, and buy only as much butter, milk, meat, and fresh fruits and vegetables as you'll cook and consume in a few days. Keep a package of pasta and a jar of gourmet sauce on hand for unexpected guests.

- Try putting a lazy Susan in the refrigerator so it's not a major project to dig through the refrigerator—and so you don't accidentally buy a duplicate just because you couldn't find something!

- To avoid duplicate purchases and things that will go bad before you use them, check your fridge items before you go grocery shopping (even before you make your grocery list).

Chapter 9

The Bacteria-Free Bathroom

Follow the bathroom-chore rule: First dry, then wet. Sweep the floor before you start working with sprays or water, so any dirt there doesn't get wet and tracked throughout the bathroom. Also bring in the vacuum and use the hose attachment on floors, corners, windowsills, and any other dirty but dry surface. It's a lot easier to empty a vacuum than to clean up hair, tissue scraps, and other debris after it's gotten wet.

Toss a rug without backing in the wash with an ordinary load.

Bathroom rugs without backings don't need special treatment; you can wash them with the rest of your laundry and tumble dry on low heat. Rugs with backing (next time buy one without) have to be washed alone in warm water and need to be air-dried. If you like, send such a rug through the drier for 10 minutes on the "fluff" or "air-dry" setting after it's mostly dry, so lint will be left behind in the lint trap.

Pair a bathtub mat with towels to get both clean.

You can wash even a mildewed rubber or vinyl bathtub mat (the kind with all those suction cups) in the clothes washer, but you'll improve the odds of it coming out clean if you add terrycloth towels to the same load. They'll rub against each other in the wash and rinse cycles, which effectively scrubs the mat clean.

Clean and Green

Baking soda is a bathroom basic. As member coordinator at the Blue Hill Co-op in Blue Hill, Maine, Toby Klein is passionately interested in making health food available to community members. Her "green" values don't stop at the bathroom door, either, which is why she uses baking soda to clean all the surfaces except the window and the mirror. "I use it in place of chemical scouring powder to get grime out of the tub or sink," she says. "I scatter some baking soda, sprinkle a little water on top, and then let it work in for a while before I scrub it off with a clean, used cloth. For chrome and tougher spots, I make a paste from baking soda and work with that." Baking soda's also handy for cleaning bathroom tiles. Just sprinkle some on, scrub it off with a damp cloth, and wipe clean with a damp mop or sponge. Toby says you can use a no-name brand soda if you want to save a few coins. "Any brand will do, because it's not like you're baking with a teaspoon of soda and really need the precisely formulated stuff."

*

Use a bucket instead of the sink or tub.

Conventional wisdom says to clean the tub or sink last, so you can use it as a makeshift container for your cleaning suds in the meantime. The truth is, it's much more time-consuming to wash a grimy ring from the tub or sink than it is to use a bucket for detergent and rinse water. Make sure you fill the bucket just half-full, though, so you can walk it outside to dump without sloshing. The water from a bucket can be easily reused, too—dump it on the compost if it doesn't have no-no chemicals in it. Or, if it's mostly dirty water and dishwashing detergent, use it to water plants you have cleverly planted below the bathroom window.

Time-Saving Supplies

Keep a dish brush with an 8- to 10-inch (20- to 25-cm) handle with your bathroom-cleaning supplies. Available on the detergent aisle at any grocery or discount department store, the tough bristles and extra reach on a dish brush will help you scrub bathroom tiles and reach awkward spots—behind the toilet, say, or in tight corners on the tub.

✳

Kill mold or mildew on tile or grout with chlorine bleach. Mix one part bleach and two parts water in a labeled spray bottle you reserve just for this purpose. The surface should be dry before you start, and test a small, hidden spot first to make sure you're not going to harm the finish. Then spray the mold or mildew with the bleach concoction, let it sink in for 10 to 15 minutes, scrub it with a brush, and rinse thoroughly. Don't breathe in the bleach, and keep the area well-ventilated while you work and for several hours after. If you are uncomfortable using bleach, try a commercial oxygenated cleaner such as Bio-OX Citrus Concentrate.

Scour your tub, clean your broom.

If it's awkward to get on your hands and knees to move scouring powder around the bottom of the tub, try sweeping it down toward the drain with a broom before rinsing with a hand-held shower set to a strong spray. Then rinse the ends of the broom, and it will get clean at the same time as the tub.

Time-Saving Supplies

Use liquid laundry detergent to clean grimy tubs. If your tub's fairly grubby, swab it down with a sponge and a glug of liquid laundry detergent in a gallon of water. Let it sit for a while before scrubbing and rinsing, and then repeat if you need to. That will get the tub back on this side of health department standards, and it may take some hard-water discoloration off the tub walls, too.

Skip the used toothbrush. Of course it's handy to have a small brush to scrub grout between tiles and such, but it shouldn't be one that was previously used on human teeth. That's just an invitation to spread germs! Instead, buy new toothbrushes at the dollar store, and soak the ends in hydrogen peroxide and rinse thoroughly with boiling water between uses.

Bleach out grime and mildew. When grime and mildew don't respond to regular household cleaners, try this bleach solution. Combine equal parts water and household bleach. Bleach kills mildew and removes many stains. Scrub the solution into the filthy tile with a grout brush or a stiff-bristled new (not used!) toothbrush. Leave the bleach solution on for a few minutes after scrubbing, then rinse away with clean water. For tougher mildew stains on grout, use the toothbrush. Apply a tile-cleaning solution with the brush, and scrub the problem area. Let it sit for a couple of minutes, then scrub clean, taking care not to loosen any grout.

*

Sock it to soap scum in the shower with orange cleaner. Mist the shower with a commercially prepared orange cleaner, such as 409 Orange Power. Give it 10 minutes to dissolve the dirt before wiping it off with a heavy-duty paper towel, such as Brawny, or a clean towel. If your job is tougher than that, use a different brand of concentrated orange cleaner, but don't dilute it. Pour a good amount on a clean dishrag or towel and wipe it all over the shower walls and doors. Every 30 minutes or so, come back and see if the cleaner is starting to dissolve the soap scum, and push any cleaner that's dripped down back up. When you can easily move some of the soap scum with your fingernail, scrub the surface with a sponge and maybe a little baking soda to provide abrasion without scratching. Rinse and wring the sponge frequently, and reapply the concentrated orange cleaner a second time if need be.

10 Minutes of Prevention

✔ Use a tape roll to combat slimy soap buildup. When you've used up a roll of transparent tape, slip the empty plastic ring under your soap bar in the soap dish. The air circulation will help the soap dry instead of getting mushy.

✔ Or place a sponge on the bottom of your soap dish to absorb excess water. That will keep the soap from becoming a soft, slimy mess. Just make sure to rinse and wring out the sponge every couple of days.

✔ Add 1/4 cup (55 g) of baking soda to your bathwater. You'll never notice it, but it should keep a ring from forming.

✳

To avoid soap-scum buildup, switch to a natural or liquid soap.
"Talc in most bar soaps causes the soap scum," says Jenny Hall, a registered nurse and avid natural soapmaker in Knoxville, Tennessee. "It won't build up like that if you use handmade soaps made with glycerin or lye." Liquid soaps are engineered to flow freely, not stick, so they'll work to prevent soap scum, too.

✳

To remove deposits on your showerhead, try vinegar. Unscrew the showerhead and soak it in warm vinegar in a heavy-duty resealable plastic bag for at least 10 hours or overnight.

To do in hard-water stains on your shower doors, thoroughly clean with a de-limer product such as Lime-A-Way. That the advice of Louise Kurzeka, who with Pam Hix co-owns Everything's Together. Though the firm specializes in clutter counseling, the two do veer into cleaning when it affects household operation. And to keep those stains from coming back, Louise says, "apply a rain-guard finish ordinarily used on windshields, such as Rain-X. This will help the water sheet off more smoothly."

✳

Try these four ways to keep your shower cleaner and brighter.

1. Seal fiberglass or glass doors with car wax to protect them from hard-water spots. Twice a year, apply a product such as Turtle Wax on the walls and doors, following the directions on the container. The finish will make it easier to wipe the doors clean, too.

2. Remove the lingering water that causes mildew with a small squeegee. It just takes an extra minute to pull a squeegee down the shower walls and doors after you've finished showering.

3. If your shower curtain dips into the bathwater, cut a couple of inches off the bottom to keep it from mildewing as quickly.

4. Rearrange the curtain rod. If you have a shower curtain/tub arrangement and water somehow seems to always spray out of the shower and onto the bathroom floor, buy an L-shaped curtain rod and use two shower curtains side by side. Instead of installing the short end of the L opposite the shower head, however, put it on the wall below the shower head.

Skip the shower spray unless you don't really need it. Even the manufacturer will tell you that those pricey daily "shower sprays" will only work if you start out with a clean stall in the first place—not very helpful for most of us! If you do fall into that category, it's still cheaper and easier to make your own from common household ingredients so you can replace it at will. If you run out of the commercial product, which is supposed to be used every day, you'll gum up the works. Make your own by mixing one part bleach to three parts water, adding a tablespoon of white vinegar, and dispensing it from a dollar-store spray bottle.

10 Minutes of Prevention

To prevent the lingering water that grubs up the tub, mix a cleaning cocktail. To keep bath water from draining slowly, banish buildup in your drainpipes. Once a month, pour a cup (220 g) of baking soda down the drain of an empty tub, followed by a cup (235 ml) of white vinegar. After an hour, flush with warm water. The results may not be obvious right away, but you'll be blasting away the buildup that causes slow drains. This will work in the bathroom sink, too, although it just gets rid of soap and grease buildup, not hair.

Machine-wash a plastic shower curtain. First, though, while it's still hanging up, spray it with an orange-based all-purpose cleaner such as 409 Orange Power and let it work for about 10 minutes. Then take it down and put it in the washer with a load of towels and run it on a warm, short cycle with about half the amount of detergent you'd ordinarily use. Hang it to dry—where else?—on the shower-curtain rod.

Buy plastic liners, not shower curtains. If you know you won't take the time to scrub or wash plastic curtains, save a few bucks and just buy plastic shower-curtain liners. You can buy them in clear or translucent, which goes with most bathroom decors, or in a pastel shade to match or complement your bathroom's color scheme. When they get mildewy or grimy, you can just take them down and toss them.

*

Skip the blue water. Blue water and disposable toilet scrubbers offer mostly mental health benefits. Jenny Hall is a registered nurse at University of Tennessee Student Health Services, and plenty of the patients she sees are probably living in less than perfectly hygienic dorm rooms. But those tabs that turn the toilet bowl blue don't do much to bring a bathroom up to health standards, she says. "They mostly just turn the water a reassuring color." Same with those toilet brushes that have disposable tips. "Unless you're in a commercial or business setting, all your toilet probably needs is a weekly brush with a product such as Lysol Toilet Bowl Cleaner," says Jenny. For use at the home she shares with daughter Laurel and husband Roger, Jenny does like the reusable toilet brushes that snap into a plastic base, however. "It's very unlikely that anything on a toilet brush will make you ill after it's been in the same water with toilet bowl cleaners," she says. "But it's nice not to have to touch the brush at all."

*

Don't forget the toilet seat. More than the color of your toilet water, be concerned with wiping the top and bottom of the toilet seat with a paper towel and any brand of all-purpose cleaner, such as 409, says William Mixon, MD, an internist at University of Tennessee Student Health Services in Knoxville. "That will basically kill any germs you would need to worry about," he says. For aesthetic purposes, make sure to give the area at the base of the toilet and between the tank and the hinge of the toilet seat a swipe with the paper towel, too.

Proceed with Caution

Go easy on your lungs with these precautions:

✓ **Never mix chlorine-based products with ammonia-based products.**
Read labels carefully so you're never using solutions with bleach at the
same time as ones that include ammonia. The two together release
chlorine gas, and if you breathe it in, you can seriously burn your mouth,
nose, air passages, and lungs. Use one or the other, but never both
together.

✓ **Ventilate when you clean with chlorine products.** Ironically, just as
mildew is hard on allergy sufferers, the chlorine-based products that
eradicate mildew can be hard on the old breathing apparatus. "Make
sure you have ample ventilation before using any product with bleach or
concentrated amounts of chlorine," says Jenny Hall. "Even better, use
products like Tilex right before you go to bed, close the bathroom door
for the night, and open a window or turn on the fan, if you have one."

*

When water deposits build up around the faucet, haul out the vinegar.
Soak a heavy-duty paper towel in white vinegar and place it around the
faucet so that it's in contact with the water deposits. Let it sit for several
hours, then remove the paper towel and scrub the deposits with a
kitchen brush or white-bottomed sponge. Make sure to dry the area
right afterward with a paper towel to delay the next buildup's progress.

Proceed with Caution

✓ **Do not use orange-based or powdered cleansers on brass or gold-plated faucets.** These fixtures corrode and scratch quickly. Instead, rub them with a lemon wedge dipped in salt to clean them, and dry them with a towel after each use. And with all that hassle, try to remember never to install such fixtures again when the choice is yours.

✓ **Chemicals can hurt chrome.** Commercial cleaning solutions can etch or scratch chrome. Instead, try a peroxide-based cleaner such as Bio-OX Citrus Concentrate or an acid-based cleaner such as vinegar or lemon juice. Dip a soft cloth into the cleaner, apply it to the chrome, and let it work for a few minutes. Rinse it with clean water, and then rub it dry with a lint-free cloth such as a diaper to restore the shine. Another solution for stains on chrome: Use a few drops of baby oil and rub it to a shine with a lint-free towel or cloth diaper. Works on tile, too!

*

Use shaving cream to keep the bathroom mirror fog-free. Wipe a layer of the white, foamy kind over the mirror, and then wipe it away with a soft cloth. Repeat when you notice that the mirror is starting to fog again. If you need the mirror to be defogged right this minute, point a hair dryer at it and turn it to hot. It'll clear up fog as fast as a car windshield defroster.

*

Have at hair spray with rubbing alcohol. Wipe hair-spray splashes from the bathroom mirror or tiles with a cloth dampened with rubbing alcohol. Another solution is to borrow a bit of shampoo touted as "daily clarifying" from the shower. Just use a dot of it with some water, and dry the mirror or tiles thoroughly afterward.

Make over your medicine cabinet in minutes. Try this six-step process to clear the junk out of your medicine cabinet for good.

1. First, take out the medicines and never put them back. Never mind what the cabinet's called; it's too hot and humid for meds in there, and all those little bottles you should have thrown out years ago are just taking up space. Toss what's expired and anything that doesn't have some sort of date. Seal the rest in a Tupperware-type container and store it in a cool, dry place like your bedside table.

2. Dump any toothbrushes that don't have a clear owner or are more than three months old.

3. Toss any cosmetics that are more than six months old or that you never use, and also get rid of any spray pumps and aerosol hair sprays that aren't in good working order.

4. Clean glass medicine cabinet shelves with a little white vinegar and water on a soft cloth. Rub the dirt off and dry the shelf at the same time. Do the same thing with metal shelves, only sprinkle a bit of baking soda on the shelves and wipe them clean with a clean, damp cloth.

5. Use a clean rag dipped in vinegar to wipe grit and grime from any containers you plan to restore to the cabinet, then dry them with a soft, clean cloth.

6. Restock the cabinet with only those toiletries that are current and have caps, and that you use at least once a day: shaving cream and a razor, for example.

10 Minutes of Prevention

Ring around your toilet bowl? Alkaline water is the culprit. Once you get it scrubbed off really well, prevent a reappearance by pouring a cup (235 ml) of white vinegar in the bowl once a month. Let it sit for several hours and flush.

Chapter 10

The Better-Kept Bedroom

Don't forget the hidden dusty spots. Since you breathe in any dust in the bedroom continuously every night while you sleep, it's worth every second to seek out the odd spots and keep them dusted. That would include the back of the headboard (pull out the bed and check), the back of the bedroom television (with its oh-so-dust-attractive static electricity), and those dust bunnies under the bed, which you can swipe out with a dust mop or a clean sweat sock on the end of a broom handle. Also dust off any ceiling-light fixtures or fans, and run a slightly damp, soft cloth across the tops of door jams and doors.

*

Reduce pickup time in the bedroom. If you use your bedroom as kind of a relaxation headquarters, lots of nonbedroom stuff tends to end up all over the place—and that's not even counting those sweatpants on the floor! Here are ways to reduce the clutter so you can spend your 10-minute cleaning sessions actually making the place cleaner:

✔ **"Loan" yourself books for nighttime reading.** To clear up that stack of bedside reading that could come crashing down any second and always seems to have water rings from your beverage, store the books elsewhere and "check out" just one at a time to read in bed. Make it a rule that you have to replace one book or magazine on the shelf before you can have another.

✔ **Put a tray on the floor at the door, room service-style.** That way, you can transport all the dirty dishes littering your room when you leave it in the a.m.—not just the two you can carry in your hands. Carry the tray back from the kitchen when you retire for the evening.

✔ **Buy a really nice travel mug—but only one.** And then use it exclusively for beverages in the bedroom. Not only will you cut down on the number of moldy coffee cups littering the place, but you're less likely to splash your beverage of choice on the carpet on trips back and forth from the kitchen.

✔ **Use a reading light that attaches to your book.** If you do, you may be able to get rid of the nightstand and bedside lamp altogether. (And as we all know, nightstands are notorious clutter traps.)

✔ **Hang the hanger from your morning outfit on the closet doorknob.** Then if your outfit's still clean, hang it up again when you undress in the evening (try to make it a habit to do this in front of the closet). If it's not clean, replace the hanger in the closet, and you'll never again see it thrown on the bedroom floor.

*

Let the cleaning product fit the bed. Give brass and varnished beds a lift with lemon oil. Dust first, and then rub them lightly with a dab of lemon oil on a slightly damp cloth. Furniture polish is all you need for wood headboards, and an all-purpose cleaner such as 409 is good for laminates. Just make sure to do all this wiping with the bedding removed, and apply the cleaner to the cloth or paper towel instead of spraying it directly on the bed, so it doesn't get on the mattress.

*

Use a laundry softener sheet to pick up animal hair. If you can't seem to keep the cat from napping on the dresser or nightstand, use a dryer sheet to pick up the hairs quickly. If the perfume bothers you, try the scent-free type.

✳

Place a small container of waterless hand sanitizer on your night table. When you think of it, rub a little on the bedroom phone receiver and the bedroom doorknob with your fingers to keep them sanitary. Or use a disinfectant wipe, and then dry them with a paper towel.

Time-Saving Supplies

Keep a Pledge mitt, Swiffer cloth, or a microfiber cloth in a plastic bag in the night-table drawer. That way, if you have a few minutes during a commercial or while you're waiting for your coffee to cool, you can quickly dust your bedside tables, dresser, and headboard.

*

Stop harboring unnecessary jewelry on your vanity or in the jewelry box. It just attracts grime and slows you down when you're trying to get ready in the morning. Next time you have 10 minutes, pick through all your pieces, even the ones you have displayed on earring trees or other fancy gizmos, and get rid of anything that's outdated or that you never use. Make a Goodwill store or kindergarten class happy by passing along the costume jewelry discards!

*

Vacuum like a clock. Both to make sure you don't skip part of the floor and to make the most of your time, start vacuuming to the left of the bedroom door and proceed around the room in a clockwise fashion until you reach the door once more, so you can take the vacuum out with you.

*

Cut down on kids' bedroom mess. Alison Rubin co-owns a Merry Maids franchise with her husband in Boca Raton, Florida, and she'll tell you that half of keeping a kid's room clean involves careful planning. Here are a few of her tried-and-true strategies:

✔ **If your kids keep their toys in their rooms, halve the mess.** "Put away half of your kids' toys and switch them around every few months. They'll have plenty to play with, and their room will stay cleaner," Alison says.

✔ **Put hooks and pegs on the back of the kids' bedroom door.** Then make it a rule that they head straight for the bedroom to hang up their backpack, jacket, and so forth when they first get home. "Hooks on the inside of closet doors are a good idea, too," she adds.

✔ **Buy a hanging shoe organizer and a CD holder.** "That keeps your kicks and tunes within arm's reach," Alison says. And the kids won't tear up the house looking for either one!

✔ **Let kids listen to loud music when they clean.** As Alison says, "The noise is a small price to pay for a clean room!"

So kids can put their own stuff away, make sure drawers slide easily. Even if you've got a fancy home, cardboard dressers make sense for the preteen set because they're lightweight and don't stick when the kids are trying to store clean clothes. Or try those metal-and-wicker drawer sets intended for good air flow in the kitchen (most people use them to store potatoes and onions). You could even replace the whole dresser idea with baskets or open shelves kids can reach readily.

Take heavy comforters or blankets to the Laundromat. Washing heavy bedding in your home machine can mean a costly and inconvenient broken washer at worst and improperly cleaned covers (the soap and water don't reach into the folds) at best. Instead, invest your 10 minutes in driving time and take those heavy covers to the Laundromat.

Proceed with Caution

Keep sheet allergens to a minimum. Sometimes a renewed enthusiasm for washing your sheets more frequently can instigate allergy attacks. So take heed: Use 1/4 cup (60 ml) of white vinegar in the final rinse to soften sheets instead of using dryer sheets if you're allergic to some perfumes. See if you don't breathe easier (without sacrificing softness). And no matter how cozy they look in the catalog, avoid flannel sheets if you're an allergy sufferer, because they produce more lint. You can buy them at yard sales, though, because the lint gradually wears down to ordinary sheet levels after repeated washings.

*

Dry a comforter or bedspread with a clean canvas sneaker or two tennis balls. Superior to an "air fluff" drier cycle, the pounding will puff up the fluff inside a comforter. The same technique works for polyester-fill pillows, but you have to dry them one at a time.

✳

Wash polyester and poly-blend sheets in warm water. No need to blast sheets with hot water unless they're 100 percent cotton—the polyester actually comes cleaner at milder temperatures.

✳

Try bath salts for bedding. If allergies aren't an issue and you particularly like the scent of your bath salts (or always receive them as gifts and never use them), use them to scent sheets and machine-washable light-weight blankets and bedspreads. Just add about 1/4 cup (50 g) to the final cycle of the wash.

*

Every few months, flip the mattress. This will not only help it wear more evenly, but it will give you a chance to vacuum the crumbs and debris that invariably slip below the sheets, between the mattress and box springs, and behind the bed. The first time, flip it side to side, and the next, flip it end over end, and then keep alternating. If you're talking about a queen- or king-size mattress, it's not an involved job, but it will require a buddy to help. First, pull the bed far enough away from the wall so that you can stand between it and the wall to tug and flip. Then strip the mattress of all covers, and vacuum the top with a Dustbuster or upholstery attachment on an ordinary vacuum. Lift the top mattress a few inches on one end and slide a large plastic garbage bag (or plastic dry-cleaning bag) between it and the box spring. With a mighty tug, pull the mattress toward you and away from the plastic insert and ease it until it is standing on its end on the plastic. Then lower the mattress (with a helper to steady it if it's big) to the flip side, ease the plastic out, and push the mattress back into place.

Make your bed in minutes. The simplest way to make your bedroom look neater is, duh, making the bed every morning. Not only is it tidier, but you won't lose things, like the remote, in the covers, and you won't be tempted to toss stuff on top like you would on a clean table, because you know you need to climb back under the covers come evening. To make the job easier, try these tactics:

✔ **Buy a sheet-material duvet.** Duvets—those things that button or zip over your comforter and then come off readily to be tossed in the wash—come in all-cotton varieties, and several types have sheeting material on one side and comforter material on the other. "They can be pricey, but if you buy the right kind, you can do without the top sheet on your bed, which is especially handy for kids," says Cathy Steever, a mother of four and a staff manager at a mail-order company that sells all kinds of quality bedding in the Boston area.

✔ **Gradually get bigger bedcovers.** If you have a full-size bed, buy a queen-size comforter, and use a full-size comforter for twin beds. The extra inches will save lots of time when you're smoothing the comforter over what's beneath. If the expense is too great, switch out gradually by, say, moving one of the full-size bed comforters to a twin bed and purchasing a larger bedspread for the full-size bed.

✔ **Buy a couple of extra pillows and cover them with shams.** These are not to lay your head on, so get the least expensive ones you can find. Cover them with attractive shams and toss them on top of your sleeping pillows in the morning when you make your bed: It takes much less time than smoothing the bedspread over the pillows, and you won't have to wash them very often because no one will be sleeping on them.

✳

Freshen a musty mattress with baking soda. After you strip the covers and sheets, sprinkle a thin layer of baking soda on top. Let it sit for a few hours, sweep up what you can with a whisk broom and dustpan, and vacuum up the rest.

Skip the bedroom clothes hamper. It may keep laundry out of sight, but it doesn't smell very good, and it's a common clutter magnet. (How long has it been since you've seen the top of your hamper lid? Or the bottom of the hamper?) Instead, toss dirty clothes into a laundry basket in the hall and take them to the laundry room in the morning. Depending on how frequently you run a load, put them directly into the washer, or separate them into appropriate piles in more baskets that you keep near the washer for that purpose.

10 Minutes of Prevention

Stop the stink in sports shoes. Whether the well-used workout shoes belong to you, the man of the house, or an active teenager, stinky sports shoes can make the whole bedroom smell bad. A product such as Bac-Out is helpful after the fact, but it's much quicker to prevent the stink in the first place than to spend a lot of time cleaning the shoes and everything they've been stored with. If you follow these steps, you shouldn't have to resort to throwing superstinky shoes away nearly so often, either:

✓ Make sure to wear socks with sports shoes.

✓ Don't put your socks in the shoes for storage: The two will transfer odors to each other, and the moisture will turn into mildew in such close quarters.

✓ Don't let the shoes end up at the bottom of the inevitable pile of clothes on the bedroom floor, or they'll never dry out. In fact, don't cover moist shoes with anything, even the inside of a gym bag. Let them stay out in the open air, on the porch if necessary, but not outside in the moist night air.

✓ If you or your child wears athletic shoes a lot, make sure you have two pairs. Then one can dry while you use the other.

*

Clean stuffed animals carefully. You don't have to be resigned to a grimy Binky or other stuffed animals. Instead, follow these cleaning instructions from Alison Rubin, who co-owns a Merry Maids franchise with her husband in Boca Raton, Florida. "If a toy animal is stuffed with natural fibers, it should not be immersed in water, but you can wipe it off with a soapy cloth, followed by a clean, wet cloth," she says. "Make sure the animal doesn't have a sound box or other mechanical parts or torn seams before you put it in the washing machine." If an animal passes those tests, Alison says to put it in a pillowcase, tie a knot in the top to keep the pillowcase closed, and wash it in the washing machine on gentle cycle. "You can also freshen stuffed animals by closing them in a paper sack with a handful of baking soda and shaking them up good."

Chapter 11

The Clean, Organized Home Office

Treat your home office like the real office. If more than one person shares the computer, desk, or telephone, sanitize your home office the same way you would if you were at a site outside the home to keep from spreading germs and flu. "I keep a can of orange disinfectant wipes in my desk, and about once a week or when one of those people walks in and says, 'I think I'm coming down with the flu,' I wipe down the phone, doorknobs, and desktop," says Joy Brooks, the deputy clerk for the Commissioner of Revenue for Smyth County, Virginia. "That keeps down germs and leaves it smelling like I've spent hours cleaning." An important aspect of this approach is to keep the wipes right in the office, not with your household cleaning supplies, so they're convenient if you're sitting down immediately after another office user—and you don't have to hunt them down if you have a few minutes while you're stuck on hold.

Clean and Green

Clean the telephone with a soft cloth dipped in white vinegar. Even grime will give in if you rub hard enough. And dip a Q-tip in vinegar for the awkward spots between push buttons. Don't worry, the smell dissipates quickly but the clean stays.

Recycle paper somewhere else. While conventional wisdom might dictate a second trashcan near your home-office printer for discarding recyclable paper, you're much better off saving it with the other household recycling materials in another room—or even in the garage or basement. That's because the paper pulp can put particles in the air, and the last thing you want is more dust near your computer. Plus, you're more likely to forget to put it out for collection if it's not with the other stuff. So each time you leave the home office, take your recyclable paper with you.

Once-a-Year Wonders

Pare away piles of paperwork. Though it took Knoxville, Tennessee, estate attorney Anne McKinney hours and hours to clear the paperwork from her home office, she used a tactic that can be broken into 10-minute increments: divide and conquer. "I based this on a clutter-conquering book I'd read, but I adapted it for my purposes," says Anne. "I brought five big boxes up to the office and marked them Keep, Shred, Nostalgia, Give Away, and Maybe. Then I put a good book on tape in my headset and dropped everything into one of the boxes." Once you have such boxes in order, you could do the same thing 10 minutes at a time, says Anne. "After that initial phase, it was easy enough to shred what needed to be shredded and give away what needed to go other places. As for the Maybe box, I put all that in a file cabinet while watching an adventure movie with my husband. I made sure to rent something I'd already seen, but he hadn't, so I could have the company but not really need to pay attention to the movie if the task got more absorbing."

*

Upend the keyboard. Most debris in a keyboard will tumble right out if you unplug it and turn it upside down. Give it a firm tap, too, to dislodge any stubborn particles.

*

Clean your keys. Dampen a paper towel or cloth rag with 80 or 90 percent rubbing alcohol and use it to wipe down your keyboard and the tops of its keys, but only after unplugging it. Stay away from commercial cleaners like 409 for this job, since they tend to leave a residue that attracts dirt.

Proceed with Caution

Always turn off your PC and monitor and unplug before cleaning. Just a drop of cleaning fluid where you don't want it can totally disrupt sensitive electronics. And never spray directly onto the hardware. Instead, spray the cloth or sponge and use that to wipe the PC clean.

Clean the keyboard with compressed air. To save time and wear and tear on your keyboard, follow the example of Ellen Robinson, an executive assistant at Siemens Medical Solutions USA. She always uses a can of compressed air, purchased at an office-supply store, "to blow all the dust and crumbs out of the keyboard." Just make sure to follow the safety instructions on the can, says Ellen and make sure you have plenty of ventilation. Then release the air in a series of short blasts, since a lengthy shot may cause condensed moisture to form on your PC.

A mini-vacuum can give maxi results. If you just can't help noshing while you surf the Internet or use TurboTax, consider buying a small computer vacuum. It will save you from hauling out the big vac to get up a few potato-chip crumbs, and it costs just a little over $10. You can use a mini-vacuum to remove dust from the interior of your computer, too, especially from wires, chips, and circuitry, where it can act like an insulating blanket and cause the PC to overheat, never a good thing.

Proceed with Caution

Monitor monitor-cleaning products. It's easy to get that dust off your monitor case—just unplug it and clean it off with a clean cotton cloth moistened with water, then dry it with a second clean cotton cloth. The screen can be dusted with a dry cloth, too. Skip the temptation to go one better with a glass cleaner: Manufacturers warn against them, principally because they contain ammonia, which can mar the screen. If you simply must get a cleaning solution, buy one specifically recommended in your owner's manual. And never use any kind of furniture polish on a computer monitor, because the fumes can be combustible.

＊

Clean your mouse, or just its pad? Unless it's misdirecting your cursor, there's no need to clean the mouse. Instead, use some diluted rubbing alcohol and a lint-free cloth to wipe down the mouse pad, which will quickly amass dirt and oil and transfer them to the mouse. But if your mouse is skipping, sticking, and even refusing to move, shut down the PC and unplug the mouse, turn it over, and remove the ring on the bottom to free the roller ball inside. Extract any gunk from the two plastic rollers inside using the end of a paper clip or tweezers, making sure to rotate them as you work. Then blow inside the cavity to dislodge any other puffs of dust or lint. Wash the roller ball with a little warm water (use a light touch of hand soap if it's grimy), dry it, and replace it and the ring on the bottom. Hook everything back up, and the mouse should work fine.

＊

Don't clean an optical mouse. An optical mouse needs no cleaning. Logitech and Microsoft, for example, make numerous optical mouse models, which have no moving parts that would require cleaning.

＊

Perish the thought of Post-its. Little sticky notes everywhere might seem handy, but they look cluttered, can get grimy quickly, and they're ironically easy to miss when there are too many of them. Instead, get a big, inexpensive school notebook for notes and put it (or several) where everyone in the household can flip through it once a day. Cross out notes that are no longer current, but every now and then flip backward several pages in the book to make sure you haven't missed anything.

Corral the cords. Use a piece of foam-tube insulation to tidy a mass of cords. Just cut a lengthwise slit in a piece about 6 inches (15 cm) long, nail or glue it below your desk, and feed the cords into the tube. Small, self-adhering clips that help guide and hold cords in place are also available at office-supply stores.

10 Minutes of Prevention

These three tactics will help you be more efficient and less frustrated looking for missing office supplies.

✓ Keep dust down by putting supplies in a drawer. Instead of open containers of clips and tacks that collect grime and need to be washed, use a plastic drawer organizer inside a drawer. Or try an inexpensive plastic ice-cube tray. Stashing staplers and tape dispensers in a drawer not only keeps them from collecting dust, but it makes them much less likely to walk off with another member of the household.

✓ Don't display more than you use. Keep supplies, from rubber bands to ballpoint pens, in their original packaging and out of sight, replenishing what you need on your desk as you need it. That means fewer little objects to attract dust or spill (or to be spilled by the pets).

✓ Make a bill-paying basket. To keep all the little stuff you need to get the bills paid and mailed out together and tidy, make a portable "bill-paying kit" out of a large divided basket with a handle.

Chapter 12

A Clean Porch to Perch On

Sweep and vacuum your porch. The porch is the source of lots of dust and loose dirt, caused by everything from foot traffic to hanging baskets. Before resorting to a wet wash, sweep or vacuum what you can, starting with the outside walls, and moving inward to the inside walls, windowsills, and any doorframes and thresholds. Then sweep (or vacuum) any loose dirt from the floor before proceeding with any wet cleaning products.

Time-Saving Supplies

Corral cobwebs with a Swiffer. Ridding high corners of cobwebs is pretty simple with a broom, but then the cobwebs take up sticky residence on the end of your bristles, and they're hard to shake. Instead, if you've already got one of those Swiffer dust mops, poke it into those hard-to-reach corners, and then toss the dirty sheet and all those sticky cobwebs right into the trash.

*

Clean off concrete with the same stuff you use to get your whitest whites. These days, Jackie Castle is a marketing executive in Johnson City, Tennessee, but she paid part of her way through school by working as a lifeguard at the Tennessee Valley Authority campgrounds, where she definitely picked up lots of know-how about cleaning concrete. "If a person was hurt and blood or other wonderful bodily fluids ended up on the floor, we cleaned it with straight bleach, as soon as we could get to it," she says. "But just to clean somewhat dirty concrete, I'd dilute the bleach 50/50 with water. In either case, use a wide bristle brush and rinse it with the hose. With the bleach, it's really important to wear rubber gloves and keep the area well-ventilated-and not to get it anywhere near ammonia products."

*

If you need to rid concrete of mildew, try TSP. That's trisodium phosphate, a heavy alkaline detergent you can purchase at the home or pool store. Use about 1/2 cup (120 ml) per gallon (3.8 L) of hot water, and rinse it with the hose.

Proceed with Caution

Consider safety first before cleaning or rinsing concrete with a pressure washer. With or without a hired hand to run it for you, a rental pressure washer can make short work of mildew and mold on concrete porches if there's somewhere for the water to drain afterward. And the rental fees are usually pretty reasonable, says Wade Slate, a lawn-care professional in Knoxville, Tennessee, who also offers his customers professional pressure-washing services. "Of course, even if you use it with bleach or TSP, longtime stains may not come out completely," he notes. "But it works quite well to take off algae, mildew, mold, and just plain dirt, and usually you won't need to use any cleaning solution." But you do need to take some safety precautions. If you're using a cleaning solution, read the precautions and consider where the runoff will end up. Wear protective eyeglasses during the operation. Cover any plants in the vicinity with a tarp before you start blasting water, or they may get washed right out of the ground. To protect the machine itself, always attach the garden hose and turn it on before starting the pressure washer, to keep the washer's pump cool so it won't burn out.

＊

Make awnings mold-free. Rid canvas awnings or porch cushions of mold or mildew with a solution of 1/2 cup (120 ml) Lysol per gallon (3.8 L) of hot water. Vacuum or brush off loose dirt first, and follow the Lysol solution with a rinse of 1 cup (235 ml) distilled white vinegar and 1 cup (200 g) salt in a gallon (3.8 L) of hot water. Let the canvas air-dry completely in direct sun before putting it back in place.

＊

If upholstered porch furniture smells musty, crack open some cat-box litter. Remove the cushions and scatter about 1/2 cup (65 g) of unused litter on each, then scatter another cup (130 g) or so on the base of the furniture. Let it sit for a few hours, sweep up what you can, and then vacuum up the remainder. Believe it or not, your furniture will now smell fresh!

※

Soak woven rope furniture in a baby swimming pool. Joan Kennedy lives among dozens of restored homes in Hampton, Virginia, most built in the 1910s, with large porches and sidewalks. She spends lots of time swinging and chatting in a porch swing that's made of woven rope and a few wooden crosspieces, so keeping it clean is a must. "A couple of times a year I wash it in a baby-sized plastic swimming pool," says Joan. "I fill it up with water and add about a cup (235 ml) of bleach and a scoop of laundry detergent—about as much as I'd use to run a load of wash." She lets the rope parts soak for 10 or 20 minutes, keeping the wooden supports out of the water. She scrubs any tough spots with a vegetable brush, and then removes the swing and rinses it off with the hose. "You want to take it out of the bleach pretty fast or you'll damage it," she says, noting that the same cleaning method would work very well for most rope hammocks.

✳

Touch up scuffs and stains on plastic furniture. Use touch-up paint for the task. The best is Krylon Fusion, a top-selling spray paint that bonds directly to most plastics without sanding or priming and dries in 15 minutes or faster. It also comes in twenty-eight colors and features the easy-to-use Touch Fan spray nozzle.

✳

Clean plastic furniture with washing soda. Washing soda (sodium carbonate) is also known as soda ash, and you can find it in the laundry section at the supermarket. Add about 1/2 cup (110 g) to a gallon (3.8 L) of hot water to make a cleaner for plastic lawn furniture. Be sure to wear gloves—the washing soda can really dry your hands—and then swipe the soda water all over the furniture with a clean towel or rag. Let it work its magic for 10 minutes, then rinse it off with the hose or wipe it down with a damp sponge, rinsing and wringing it often. If the stains refuse to budge, repeat the process, but this time, leave the soda water to soak in for 20 minutes.

Protect plastic furniture with car wax.

A coating of car wax ensures that the furniture requires no more than a quick damp wipe with plain water to stay clean. Car wax also keeps most plastic furniture from fading in the sun.

Clean and Green

Try tea tree oil to clean mildew and mold. You can find tea tree oil in the health food store, and while it's fairly expensive per ounce, a little goes a long way. It's an environmentally friendly way to take mold and mildew off outdoor furniture cushions if you can handle the strong scent. (See if you can smell it in the store—it's pungent the same way menthol is, though the smell itself is different.) Mix 2 teaspoons (10 ml) with 2 cups (475 ml) of water in a spray bottle, and spot-test it on a hidden place to make sure it won't discolor your cushion. Then spray it on the cushions and . . . just leave it there. It will take a couple of days, but both the mold and the smell of tea tree oil will go away.

Skip the bleach on porch-furniture cushions. Usually, the manufacturer's label recommends against using bleach or any product that contains bleach, and you should also avoid them just to be on the safe side if you've lost your label: Bleach makes colors run and can cause spots and wearing. Instead, use an oxygen-based liquid cleaner such as Bio-OX Citrus Concentrate with Bubble Up Technology. Dilute it to one-quarter strength with water, put it in a spray bottle, and spritz the fabric you wish to clean. Then leave it alone for 10 minutes to give it time to work before wiping it off with a damp cloth. Remove any stains that remain by sprinkling them with baking soda and scrubbing with a damp scouring pad (test for scratching on a hidden piece of cushion, first), then rinsing well with water.

10 Minutes of Prevention

Make porch-furniture cushions low maintenance with some savvy purchases, a few stitches, and a little legwork:

- Keep seat cushions from mildewing by keeping them indoors. Bring them inside if rain is expected so they won't absorb mildew-causing moisture, and store them in a cool, dry place in the off-season.

- If you can't remove seat cushions to toss in the wash, make some covers. Nothing fancy, just "wrap" each cushion in a piece of thin, washable canvas or tight-weave toweling and sew Velcro strips to the fabric so that you can attach the flaps the same way you'd secure gift wrap with cellophane tape. Put the Velcro-visible side on the bottom, next to the chair frame. Then you can wash the cushion "wraps" to keep the cushions clean and fresh. Easy!

- If you purchase seat cushions, particularly at a yard sale, make sure the zippers are nylon. Metal zippers rust, which makes the cushion covers impossible to remove, which makes it very hard to keep them clean.

Keep wicker furniture clean with the hose. It's hard to imagine, but the best thing for wicker furniture is to turn the hose on it every few weeks when it's in use outdoors or on a screen porch. Just set it on the grass and rinse it with plain water. Remember to rinse the back and underside, too, and let it air-dry. If you've already got too much grimy dirt on your wicker furniture for that simple approach, dip a soft scrub brush in a mix of a quart (946 ml) of water and a tablespoon (15 ml) of Murphy's Oil Soap, scrub the wicker piece lightly, and then rinse with the hose. You can ordinarily purchase Murphy's Oil Soap at a family dollar or discount department store, or pay a little more for it at the grocery store. To prevent wicker furniture from wearing out quickly if it's on an exposed porch, try to remember to cover it with a tarp or vinyl cover when it rains.

✳

Soft Scrub scuff marks from aluminum outdoor furniture. Other scouring powders will scratch, but a little Soft Scrub on a damp, soft cloth will pick up those odd scuff marks aluminum chairs and tables are prone to.

✳

Use sandpaper to remove rust on wrought-iron outdoor furniture. Go over the rust lightly with fine-grade sandpaper, and then wipe off the debris with a clean, dry cloth. If you don't like how it looks after the rust is gone, use the manufacturer-provided touch-up paint, or head for the hardware store and see what they can set you up with.

✳

Keep ants off glass tabletops. If you serve lots of lemonade or sugary coffee from solid-surface tabletops on the porch, make sure to wipe them down often with undiluted white vinegar. The smell will dissipate after an hour or so, but it will keep ants off the scent of sugar for days.

Choose plants for hanging baskets carefully. Even if you hate to sweep up fallen petals and flowers, you can still have beautiful blooms in hanging baskets on your porch, as long as you choose the plants with care. "Create baskets using mostly foliage plants like gray helichrysum, burgundy or chartreuse ornamental sweet potato vine, or caladiums," says Barbara Pleasant, an avid gardener and garden writer in Pisgah Forest, North Carolina. "Then add colorful cascading annuals that shed very little, such as calibrachoa. Impatiens and verbena look great in hanging baskets, but they are heavy shedders."

Painted wood prevents plant-pot rings. Barbara Pleasant is also intimately familiar with the inevitable marks left by porch and deck plants, both as a gardener and as author of *The Complete Houseplant Survival Manual*. "No matter what you do, there will be rings (or footprints from pot supports) beneath porch and deck plants, because dirt from air and rain naturally accumulates there," she says. "The rings clean up easily from painted surfaces, but not so easily from stained wood. Instead of setting pots on a stained deck, paint a board with two coats of outdoor enamel, and use it as a sitting pad for pots."

Chapter 13

Tidy Exits, Entries,
and Hallways

Remember where you come in. It's fine to keep a grand entrance up front, complete with scrubbed porch and polished railings, but if everyone enters through, say, the kitchen or side door, that's where you should concentrate your cleaning efforts. Be especially sure to put a doormat wherever the people you consider "family" enter the house, and shake it out and/or sweep under it at least once a week.

＊

Nylon mats net dirt. If you've got real dirt, avoid those frou-frou light-weight woven mats with kitty cats and clever sayings. Instead, go for a sturdy nylon mat, available at discount department stores and home stores. "A good-quality, absorbent mat at the front door will cut the floor-cleaning routine in half," says Anne L. Williams, who has crossed hundreds of thresholds in the rain and snow as a realtor for Coldwell Banker Wallace & Wallace in Knoxville, Tennessee. If your yard has poor drainage, or a lot of outdoor athletes traipse through your doors, consider putting one heavy-duty mat inside and one out, and invest in a supersize mat for whichever doorway has the most traffic, particularly of the four-footed or under-eighteen variety.

✳

Give the front a once-over with Windex. Realtor Anne Williams knows all about last-minute ways to make a house look more appealing to potential buyers. A quick spruce-up at the entrance requires little more than Windex and a cloth. "Windex gives a fast sparkle to chrome, glass, and most metal fixtures," she says.

✳

Use baby powder to combat sand while you're still outside. Whether you've taken a trip to the beach or you walk through dunes to get to your backyard, sand can coat your skin. To avoid bringing it into the house to penetrate the hall carpet and eventually make its way to the shower floor, dust yourself with baby powder while you're still outside. The sand will fall off almost magically (okay, you'll need to dust it off with your hands a bit, too) once the baby powder absorbs the moisture holding it to your skin.

10 Minutes of Prevention

Lots of the dirt that comes over your threshold can be stopped at its source—not your shoes, but the places on your lawn and driveway where the dirt hitches a ride. Try several of these preventive techniques:

- Call a contractor to aerate your lawn in the fall. You'll have much thicker grass in the spring and summer, which will drink in the excess water and prevent so much mud from forming on bald lawn spots.

- Park your car right next to the sidewalk or porch steps. If your driveway's not designed so that the driver sets foot on the sidewalk when exiting the car, back in so you step out of the car and onto a nice clean footpath— without tracking through the lawn or some oil spots on the driveway first.

- Make paths and stepping-stones for gardens and to reach bird feeders. In the spring, it's essential to be able to get to and from the newly tilled earth without walking through mud, and later in the growing season, you should be able to comfortably walk out to weed and harvest without traipsing through wet grass or earth. As for bird feeders, consider whether you'll be refilling them in the snow or mud, and make sure you'll have a place to step neatly. (Use rock salt on the stepping-stones or footpath when you do the driveway, too.)

✓ Make sure your locks and doorbell work. An inordinate amount of dirt gets on people's shoes when they have to work their way around the house to get someone to let them in.

✓ Plan a path for dog walks. Instead of reluctantly dashing out in the mud and rain so your poor pooch can do his business, plan a path that is pavement for you but still allows a vegetative spot for him to do his thing at the other end of the leash.

✳

Try a sun shower. If you live in a sandy area or have an outdoor job or a home pool, consider getting a "portable sun shower" that attaches to your garden hose and stands up on a flat surface for a pseudo-shower before you come in the house. They're available online and at home and camping stores. Make sure you buy a model that has no metal parts to corrode.

Shift Gears

Plan a different dumping ground. Take it for granted that every member of the household will shed any coats, backpacks, and shopping bags at the earliest opportunity upon entering the house. When this happens within inches of the door, it looks sloppy to visitors and also necessitates at least one more daily session to sort things out and deliver them to the proper place. To change the habit, avoid placing those snazzy "hall trees," armoires, or tables more than about 18 inches (45 cm) wide within 10 yards (9 m) of a household entrance. Instead, save the coat pegs for bedroom doors, and make a space for backpacks, books, and briefcases wherever they'll be used next, whether that's the kitchen computer center, the home office, or the bedroom. This way, you save steps and eliminate an entire area of the house you have to clean.

*

Leave your shoes, keep your mess. A licensed clinical social worker and life coach, Melanie McGhee sees clients at her home in Maryville, Tennessee, so her entrance must be both inviting for them and practical for Melanie's family of four. One tactic that works well: a light-colored shoe cubby with a beautiful piece of statuary or pottery on top. The family—but not the clients—leave their shoes inside the cubby, which really cuts down on the amount of east Tennessee clay that makes its way onto the neutral hall carpets. It also saves time during the mad morning rush, since everyone knows where to find the shoes they were wearing yesterday. If you try this, though, make sure the cubbyholes are no larger than shoe size, and that you keep something nice on top; otherwise, it's too tempting to stuff, say, soccer balls and dictionaries inside, and dump an armful of garage-sale finds on top.

*

Instead of furniture in the foyer, try mirrors and houseplants.

That's the trick used by Ellen Robinson, an executive assistant who lives in a Dutch Revival two-story house built in 1929 in Knoxville, Tennessee. "Mirrors are great!" she says. "They brighten up dark entryways and are fabulous for covering bad walls." Best of all, they don't add to the clutter and are simple to keep clean. "Plants are also easy, cheap ways to brighten up an entryway without attracting clutter," says Ellen. "Use them inside or outside. Try small planters on either side of a doorway, or bushy herbs or small trees."

*

Check the mirror, check the exit. Therapist and life coach Melanie McGhee also uses a mirror in the front entrance, but she places hers near the front door. "The way this works for me is that I am assured a glance at myself as I approach the door," says Melanie, who is also the author of a self-discovery book, *The Illumined Life*. "That is a quick reminder to smile. That smile helps me notice how welcoming my entryway feels. So if the floor needs sweeping, I see it. If the shoes are piled up, I see them. And I remember to take a few minutes to make the entry inviting again."

Once-a-Year Wonders

Sponge down the hall and stair walls. Why is it irresistible to run down an empty hall or up the stairs while running your hand over the wall? Add to that the fact that those walls are plain enough that the dirt's actually visible, and you may see a need to wash them every now and then. Luckily, it doesn't take long. Use a capful of a mild cleaner such as Murphy's Oil Soap in a gallon of warm water. A well-wrung-out sponge or lint-free cloth works well, and you shouldn't have to rinse unless you've underestimated and there are streams of dingy water running down the walls.

*

Hit hallway light switches and doorknobs with all-purpose cleaner.
Near bedrooms especially, the hall lights and doorknobs get a regular
workout, so they may need a little extra elbow grease to come clean.
That, and a bit of all-purpose cleaner such as 409, applied and scrubbed
off with a soft, clean cloth.

*

Soap away crayon marks. Alison Rubin, who co-owns a Merry Maids
franchise with her husband in Boca Raton, Florida, has seen firsthand
how many kids think the world is their canvas, particularly those nice
open hallway walls. "If the little darlings draw on your walls, clean the
crayon marks with a little concentrated dishwashing soap on a soft,
damp rag," she says.

Try chalkboard paint.

While you can't always beat them by joining them, if you want clean hall walls and brilliant child artists, consider painting a section of the hallway wall with chalkboard paint, available at most discount department stores, craft stores, and specialty paint stores. It's a lot easier to erase chalk from a chalkboard than crayon or pen from walls!

Acknowledgments

So many people gave more than 10 minutes to make this book possible, starting with my sweetie, Wade Slate, who lent his expertise and also "home tested" scores of tips. Other long-suffering friends and family members consistently came through for me even as they claimed to have no special knowledge, including Keith Anders, Joy Brooks, Jackie Castle, Joan Kennedy, Ellen Robinson, Shawn Simpson, Jim Slate, Cathy Steever, Jill Kendall Williams, and Amy Witsil. I'm particularly grateful to Susan Castle for overlooking the fact that we're only related by divorce and sharing scads of neatnik secrets, and to Jenny Hall, one of my daughters' beloved aunts, for approaching the bathroom tips with good sense and good humor and asking her supervisor, William Mixon, MD, to aid the cause. I'm just as touched by the help I received from complete strangers in brief phone calls, including Knoxville realtor Anne L. Williams, Toby Klein of the Blue Hill Co-op in Blue Hill, Maine, Tammy Wood of Extreme Cleaning in Arvada, Colorado, Carla Edelen of

Complete Cleaning, LLC in St. Louis, Matt Herd from Topeka, Kansas, and Alison Rubin, who co-owns a Merry Maids franchise with her husband in Boca Raton, Florida. Many of my "everyday experts" shared thoughts for my book freely though they write themselves, including life coach Melanie McGhee, Minneapolis clutter counselors Louise Kurzeka and Pam Hix, garden writer Barbara Pleasant and estate attorney Anne McKinney. As the mystery writers like to say, while the knowledge belongs to them, any mistakes are mine! Thanks, all!

About the Author

Rose R. Kennedy is the author of the *Family Fitness Fun Book* and has contributed to numerous tip books, including *1,001 Old-Time Household Hints*, *Cut the Clutter and Stow the Stuff* and *Shameless Shortcuts*. An avid food writer and kids' book reviewer, she regularly contributes to *Disney Adventures*, www.fineliving.com, and *The Herb Companion*. Rose lives in a nicely blended family in Knoxville, Tennessee, where she's on the board for the local Actors Coop and is a devoted pet owner, backyard bird watcher and NTN trivia player.

Also Available from Fair Winds

10-MINUTE FENG SHUI
by Skye Alexander
ISBN: 1-931412-88-X
$12.00 (£7.99)
Paperback; 248 pages
Available wherever books are sold

TURN YOUR CLUTTER INTO CASH IN JUST 10 MINUTES!

Feng shui, the ancient Chinese art of placement, can transform your love life, financial situation, health, and overall happiness. And it's easier than you think to reap the rewards of this amazing art! Just a few simple changes to your décor can result in big benefits.

• Put a vase of yellow flowers in your kitchen to increase your wealth
• Place a live plant in your bedroom to improve your love life
• Tie nine small bells on a red cord and hang it from your front door to bring happiness into your home
• Hang a mobile in a sick room to clear congestion and respiratory problems

In just ten minutes, you can revive stagnant energy and bring positive "ch'i" into your home. Feng shui has been used successfully for centuries, and these tips are the best of what feng shui has to offer. They're simple, they're fun, and they work!

Also Available from Fair Winds

10-MINTUE CLUTTER CONTROL
by Skye Alexander
ISBN: 1-59233-068-1
$12.00 (£7.99)
Paperback; 256 pages
Available wherever books are sold

THE FENG SHUI CURE FOR CLUTTER

If you think that clutter control is a fact of life, think again. With the simple tips & tricks in this book, you can learn the secrets of this age-old clutter elimination system in no time. Best-selling *10-Minute Feng Shui* author Skye Alexander shows you how to transform your environment—and in doing so, transform your life as well!

Designed with the "too-busy-to-get-organized" person in mind, *10-Minute Clutter Control* breaks down organization into easy tasks that take only minutes to perform, and will work wonders for your sense of order, not to mention your peace of mind:

• Use plants to absorb emotional and mental clutter
• Furnish your home with beds of the same size
• Use a blackboard instead of Post-Its for daily reminders
  And much more!

With *10-Minute Clutter Control*, you can throw out the bad, organize the good, and attract the new luck, love, and harmony that accompany a well-managed life.